Peter Serdyukov • Mark Ryan

The 5-Minute Lesson Plan

A Practitioner's Guide

Pearson Learning Solutions, 501 Boylston Street, Suite 900,
Boston, MA 02116
A Pearson Education Company
www.pearsoned.com

Printed in the United States of America

2 3 4 5 6 7 8 9 10 v092 17 16 15

000200010271678836

ML/CB

ISBN 10: 1-256-78643-8
ISBN 13: 978-1-25678643-6

TABLE OF CONTENTS

PREFACE

The authors of the **5-Minute Lesson Plan** have undertaken a daunting task. How can we help teachers write effective lesson plans? This question leads to another: How does one convey complex notions to build a blueprint of the teaching and learning enterprise in a manner so teacher candidates will not only learn the process, but practice it? We put our knowledge and experiences in this book to make it a useful tool for teachers. To be sure, the explanation of lesson design demands knowledge and an appreciation of pedagogical practice at a very high level.

So, how do we get from here to there? To begin, there are two roads the book travels. The first journey we think you will find is a wistful and enjoyable trek of a teacher in search of a better way to instruct her students. What she finds opens the door to the rest of the book. That is where the second road begins. Unlike the first short road which takes us from a search to an answer found, the second is a road that spirals from the simple to the complex. We develop knowledge not in a straight line but in continuous, gradual, spiral motion. Note that this spiral path we used here has three levels or iterations. The first basically defines key concepts of a lesson plan, the second explains the structure and function of lesson design in detail, and the third expands the understanding of lesson planning and its implementation to make it complete and comprehensive.

Consistent effective lesson planning is essential for successful experiences in both teaching and learning. In teacher preparation, the most important goal is to prepare and educate for quality teaching in the classroom. Quality teaching, like any other occupation, requires sound rational planning, organization and management. One of the prerequisites for achieving this goal is the teacher's competence in lesson plan design which becomes an important objective in every practitioner's professional development. Lesson planning is essential in almost every aspect of daily classroom life. Good lesson plans are the foundation of successful student learning, accurate assessment, and effective classroom management. Every teacher, at some point, needs guidelines for designing quality lessons. Initial guidance in lesson plan development followed by instructional practice is the key to successful teaching.

Traditionally, planning skills have not been sufficiently developed in the teacher preparation programs or in the classroom experiences. Novice and even seasoned teachers, on being involved in the lesson planning activities, often note their lack of skills in previous educational experiences. This situation is aggravated by the expanding use of templates and ready-made lesson plans distributed by school districts. They may be good, but every teacher, in order to teach effectively, must understand how the plan is designed and learn to adapt it in the best way to his or her own unique class and real-life classroom circumstances. This is why there is an urgent need to have a text that effectively guides lesson plan development. This book combines concise and clear theoretical explanations with practical activities that help enhance user skills in designing and developing lesson plans. The text can be used by every teacher in daily practical work as a one-stop resources for designing lesson plans that encourage deep and thoughtful learning, in teacher lifelong professional development and certainly in teacher education college courses preparing future teaches for rewarding classroom experiences.

This book, originally called *Writing Effective Lesson Plans: A Five-Star Approach*, has been successfully used in teacher preparation programs in a number of universities and colleges. Candidate teachers found it very helpful in their learning and work. With time, we found it needed updates and improvements to be more useful. This is a next iteration of our approach which we offer you.

To aid in developing your **5-Minute Lesson Plan**, see the list of Internet sites below that contain state standards of all 50 states:

- **www.education-world.com/standards/state/index.shtml**
- **http://edstandards.org/Standards.html**
- **http://promethean.statestandards.com**

A QUEST

Let's "take five" and pause
before we begin. We can use
these five minutes to think
of the most important people
engaged in the thinking and learning
process—your students.

There is one other person
involved in the classroom,
you—the teacher.

You may think of yourself as a
second grade teacher or a high
school English teacher, or a Math
teacher, but what you really are is
a teacher of human beings.

CONTENTS

- The Quest

- Lesson Design

- Goals and Objectives

- Materials and Tools

- Procedures

- Assessment and Evaluation

- Time

Once upon time in a far away school that found itself surprised by the 21st century, a young teacher struggled with the realities of trying to educate students in an underfunded, unappreciated and unsuccessful school.

The young teacher was having trouble organizing her lessons. Students were bored in her class. She knew that something must be done. "I need to get my act together," she mused.

"But how can I go about that?"

Then she had an idea that seemed to come from out of nowhere.

She immediately decided, "I must go on a quest, and find out from professors and teachers how they cope with today's classroom—how they organize their teaching.

Mine will be a search far and wide over the internet, and I will keep at it until the answer is found. When it comes to teaching–I don't want to just survive—I want to thrive!"

And so the die was cast and the journey began. She searched many web sites from around the world and even emailed professors and teachers from all over the planet.

Answers, she had plenty and maybe even too many about how to teach in today's classroom:

"**D**on't smile for the first two weeks so the students know who the boss is!"

"Speak only English in the classroom to foreign students!"

"A zero tolerance policy is what today's students really need!"

"The school's mission is to prepare everyone for a job!"

Our young teacher understood the fervor of the advice, if not the wisdom.

And so her quest went on.

Other educators proclaimed:

"Bilingual education is for everyone!"

"Cooperative education models teamwork!"

"Students must become problem-solvers by using critical thinking!"

"Tell students, it is not where you line up, but where you end up!"

She liked the messages, but was not coming any closer to what she really wanted to know.

She was on a mission to find *how* to teach her class. And it looked to her like the major concern for teaching effectively was—how to structure and organize her lessons.

It was then that she heard about two elderly professors, who were friends.

Between them they had over a half-century of classroom experience from kindergarten classes to college seminars.

One was a professor from Russia, a former sergeant in the Red Army during the Cold War and then a teacher educator.

His unlikely colleague was an American professor who grew up near San Francisco, a bastion of liberal thought during the 1960s.

As vastly different as these two professors were—they did agree on one thing—*how* to organize and structure a lesson to successfully teach in the classroom of today.

Filled with both hope and trepidation (as can happen on a quest for truth), she traveled from her far away school to meet the professors.

Did they meet in the hallowed halls of the university?

No, actually when they heard she wanted to meet them they decided to take her to lunch in a Mexican restaurant.

Why not?

They sat down at the restaurant and were immediately greeted by a basket of fresh warm corn chips and a bowl of salsa.

Has anyone ever stopped at one chip?

But we digress.

She was ready to ask the question that burned within her, the question that would make her job not only easier but also help her do what great teachers do best—make a positive change in the lives of their students.

"**I** am looking for a way to become a better teacher by organizing what I do, can you help?"

"Why, of course," said the American professor, "but first we need to understand who we are teaching. Are we teaching parrots or people?"

The young teacher smiled and said, "Why, people, of course."

"**A**h," said the Russian professor, "I am glad we have made the distinction—so much of teaching today with all the so-called standardization and teaching to the test, seems more aimed at recitation —you know like..."

"Parrots," she said.

"Exactly," he intoned.

"**S**o now that we are sure we are talking about people, the first step is to write our motto!"

"A motto?" she inquired.

"Why yes, you and your students need to confront your ambiguity about the learning process. It is going to be your motto in preparing a good lesson."

"**N**ow," said the American professor, "get ready for three words that will open up the world of learning to you!

Your motto will read....."

Disposition Drives Cognition

"The idea is that how you *feel* can open or close the door to learning."

The Russian professor smiled and said, "Many will say humans are thinking beings. It is more correct to say humans are feeling beings that think!

Now, with that understanding you are ready to organize your plan for teaching like the five points of a star."

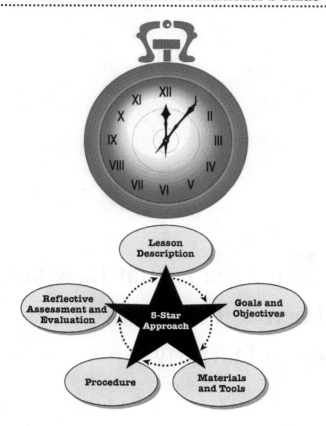

The young teacher's anticipation grew as the professors were about to tell her what she had traveled so far to hear—how to build a lesson plan.

The American began by noting, "Our secrets are imbedded in a five point star.

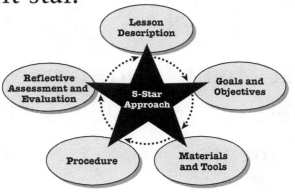

Once you understand the meaning of each point of the star—you will know within 5 minutes how to construct a lesson plan."

"Yes," said the Russian professor,— "Lessons that work wonderfully from east to west."

"That's right," added the American professor, "From Siberia to Sacramento!"

The Russian professor smiled and continued, "Before the first students come through the classroom door, a teacher must be prepared to begin the learning process based on a plan of action."

"Do you believe you need a good lesson plan to teach a good lesson?"

"Why, yes, of course," replied the teacher. "Though honestly, I don't always do so. In fact, many teachers don't write lesson plans at all."

The Russian professor exclaimed, "How unfortunate! A well-thought out lesson plan gives the teacher a sense of direction and may well foster a feeling of confidence. Think of it this way: A plan is a systematic means to reach an end."

The American professor chimed in, "Planning," as Alan Lakein said, "is bringing the future into the present so that you can do something about it now."

"That's correct," said the Russian professor, "Lesson planning is essential in almost any aspect of daily classroom life.

Good lesson plans are the foundation of successful student learning, accurate assessment, and effective classroom management.

And now you know the first corner of the 5-Star Approach."

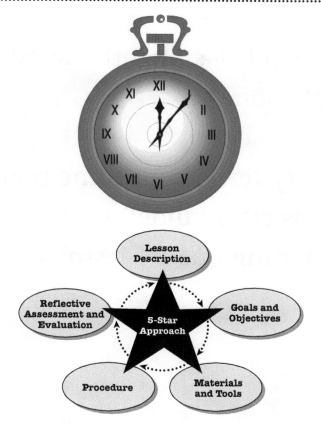

"**W**ould you like to hear about the second point of the star?" asked the American professor.

"Yes," said the young teacher. "I understand that there must be a design for each lesson, and I am guessing the other four points of the star will tell what they are."

"Precisely," stated the Russian professor.

"Every teacher, at some point, needs clear guidelines for designing quality lessons."

Effective lesson plan development followed by instructional practice is key to successful teaching.

The Russian professor continued in a professorial manner, "Any lesson has a purpose and an aim. This means every time you teach you should have clear goals and objectives.

You need to understand, however, not only where you are going in the lesson, but also what your students will accomplish in the end, which is identified in the learning outcomes."

The American professor added, "Just like a captain of a ship, knowing where you are going, what you must accomplish to get there, and how you will benefit from your voyage, a teacher must have a firm idea of how to launch a successful lesson plan."

"**O**f course," confirmed the Russian professor, "Every time you teach you should have goals and objectives at the top of your lesson plan."

The young teacher said, "I am always mixing up goals with objectives.

"Can you tell me exactly what is a goal, and how is it different from an objective?"

The American professor answered, "You are not alone in not being able to distinguish a goal from an objective.

Let me make an analogy so you never forget which is which.

"Say you want to take your class to Washington, D.C. during the Spring break. The goal is for students to see the capital city and acquaint themselves with its major sites.

To do it you should ask students to collectively develop a plan of the excursions; identify the sites they would like to see, such as Washington Monument, the Mall, Lincoln Memorial, the White House and Smithsonian Museums; prepare a presentation with demonstrations about each site; investigate how they will get to the destination and back, and compare alternative routes and means; write the expense list and calculate the costs of the travel, and finally compose an itinerary of the whole trip.

The objectives are clear and specific. The focus is on the means —preparation for the travel rather than the end—seeing Washington, D.C."

The Russian professor continued, "Thus, a **goal** is the strategic, ultimate purpose of the lesson.

An **objective** of a lesson is one of the specific, explicit, intermediate aims.

The objective also identifies the means of achieving the planned outcome."

"So," the young teacher confirmed, "The goal and objectives are actually not about what the teacher will do but about what students will achieve as a result of the lesson."

"Excellent!" exclaimed both professors.

The American professor then chimed in, "Well, you are 40 percent there, because now you know a bit about the second point of the star—goals and objectives.

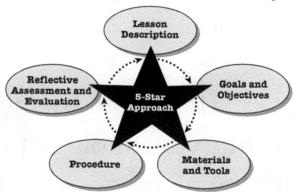

Goals and Objectives—a top right point of star

"**A**re you ready for the third point of the star?" asked the American professor.

"Sure," responded the young teacher.

He then said, "From the newest 21st century technology to traditional textbooks, the materials and tools which today's teacher can access provide a wide array of resources to enhance the learning process.

In our digital age we can see and hear video via the internet, instantaneously communicate with a cell phone, Skype or by email with a friend who is 10,000 miles away, and chat on the Facebook."

"**W**e can also access an online class virtually whenever we want and as many times as we want to reinforce learning.

Yet as our tools become more interactive, the role of the teacher does not diminish.

As a selector of what web sites to visit and as an assessor of learning, a teacher can help students explore and access virtually limitless resources in cyberspace."

The Russian professor added, "Teaching and learning require numerous materials and tools.

Tools are the teachers' and students' instruments that can be simple, such as whiteboards, pens, rulers, textbooks, and reference articles."

"**M**ore complex tools, which are referred to as educational technology, are computers, calculators, DVD players, overhead projectors, TVs, Smart Boards, and the Internet.

The right materials and tools can make for enhanced learning.

Until recently we thought only about printed texts when talking about literacy. Today we also have computer literacy, the ability to operate a computer, and visual literacy, the ability to extract or create meaning from images using electronic devices.

Today's students are more accustomed to playing computer games, scanning digital texts on the computer screen, hearing digitalized sounds in their earphones, and analyzing images on their monitor, rather than reading text printed on the paper.

Therefore, we have to integrate digital texts, sounds and images, and electronic games into teaching and learning."

"**N**o doubt, the role of electronic technology is growing in society and in the classroom, therefore we all have to know how to effectively use them in teaching and learning," said the young teacher.

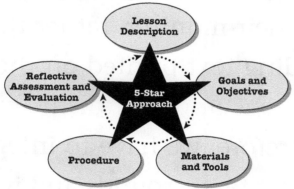

Materials and Tools are at the bottom right point of the star.

"**A**re you ready to move to the fourth part of the star?" queried the Russian professor.

"Well, this is a lot of information, but the way you explain it makes a lot of sense.

I guess I'm ready for the last two points of the star," replied the young teacher.

"Wonderful!" said the American Professor.

He continued, "Like a music conductor, the teacher must lead an orchestra according to a set plan.

There are strategies and various ways to present a lesson plan, but it is the teacher who must decide how new material is to be presented and how the students will engage with the new knowledge so that every one of them has the opportunity to achieve the planned learning outcomes."

"This is done through a special procedure which is the main part of the lesson plan," said the Russian professor.

"When implemented in the classroom, the procedure usually encompasses five major activities. They are the introduction, new material presentation, activities, assessment and evaluation, and closure.

Each lesson develops as a procedure within a preset time period."

"First of all, the teacher starts the class by introducing students to the new lesson, explaining the lesson's topic, its goal, objectives and learning outcomes.

Then the teacher may present the new material, after which students will engage in different organized activities in which they develop deep understanding of the new knowledge and corresponding skills."

"Finally, the teacher assesses and evaluates students' performance, and summarizes the lesson outcomes in a closure."

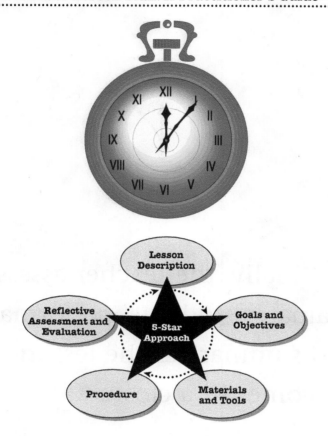

Procedure is the left point at the bottom

"**W**ell," said the young teacher, "That means only one point of the star is left—and it must do with testing my students and giving them grades."

"Part of what you say is true, testing can be helpful, but is only part of assessing your students' strengths and weaknesses, "said the American professor, "And I hope you never *give* grades.

Students *earn* grades—you, as a teacher, are merely the scorekeeper."

The Russian professor then said, "So let's talk about assessment, evaluation and reflection.

Estimating how much a student has learned gives us valuable information about the efficacy of the lesson plan and the instruction."

"To be successful, learning must be assessed and evaluated so that the student and the teacher both know the current state of the student's knowledge, skills and development.

These two terms, assessment and evaluation, are commonly confused, but believe me, there is a significant difference."

The American professor stated, "Assessment is an appraisal of the learner, which is inherently reflective.

It is based on the teacher observing a student's performance and guiding him or her towards the learning objective.

It is dynamic and continuous."

"**O**n the other hand, said the Russian professor, "evaluation is, by nature, a final judgment; it is static and represented by a grade, a rank, or a score that is a snapshot of how well a student does on a particular test on a particular day.

Assessment is directed at the future, giving the student an opportunity to improve, whereas evaluation is a finite event, after which the student may not have a chance to improve her work.

Assessment has two sides: it may be performed by the teacher, or it can be done by the students—then it becomes reflective.

Evaluation is done by the teacher or a professional evaluator using a prepared instrument, such as test, quiz, exam, or written essay.

It is critical to understand that grades should be earned by the students; they are not given by the teacher."

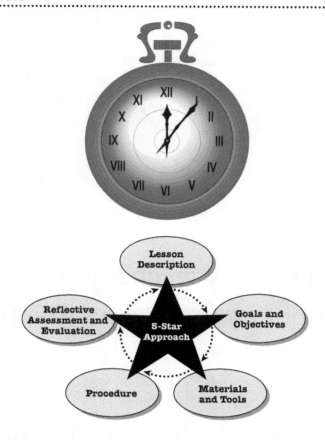

Assessment and Evaluation are the fifth point of the star on the upper left.

The young teacher looked at her cell phone to see what the <u>time</u> was.

"I guess it is <u>time</u> to go," she said. "I truly appreciate your help."

The professors nodded in response, but had one more important point to make.

The American professor said, "We have just seen how reflective assessment and evaluation are about appreciating, measuring and judging learning. These functions are an inherent part of education.

One thing you will constantly measure in the classroom is time.

Effective use of time in the lesson through time management is a sure way to achieve effective learning outcomes."

The Russian professor concluded, "Please remember as you go back to your school that time is always scarce and affects every aspect of the teaching and learning process.

Student achievement depends in great measure on the efficient use of every moment in the classroom."

"**N**ow that I know the basics of writing a five minute lesson plan using the 5-star approach, where can I continue to learn more?"asked the young teacher.

"Where does anyone find anything today?" queried the Russian professor.

"On the internet, of course!" exclaimed the American professor.

Just go to:

www.fiveminutelessonplan.com

Professors Serdyukov and Ryan ask you to join them now!

CHAPTER 1

Teaching to Performance Expectations

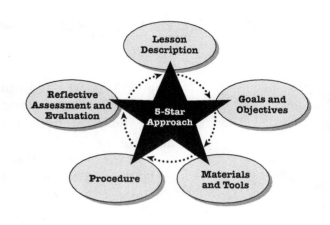

First Iteration

All teachers are expected to teach using certain standards as guidelines. Teacher preparation is also based on specific guidelines that identify essential competencies, knowledge, skills and abilities a teacher should have and be able to demonstrate. In California they are called Teacher Performance Expectations (TPEs). There are 13 TPEs grouped in six domains. TPEs can be measured using Teacher Performance Assessments (TPAs).

Teacher Performance Expectations (TPE) are the descriptions of the "knowledge, skills, and abilities beginning teachers should have and be able to demonstrate."

Teacher Performance Assessments (TPA) are instruments "designed to measure the candidate's knowledge, skills and ability with relation to California's Teaching Performance Expectations (TPEs), including demonstrating his/her ability to appropriately instruct all K–12 students in the Student Academic Content Standards.

The purpose of this edition of *Writing Effective Lesson Plans* (WELP) is to merge California TPEs and TPAs, and the plan of action summed up in the 5-Star Approach: Lesson Description, Goals and Objectives, Materials and Tools, Procedure, and Reflective Assessment and Evaluation. It would provide a pathway to students' effective learning outcomes.

Along with TPEs and TPAs a pivotal element of school education is the state standards. When preparing their lesson plans teachers have to adhere to the standards. The California State Board of Education (SBE) adopted the new Common Core State Standards on

August 2, 2010, the implementation of which will start in schools in 2013. It is a set of standards that would help prepare students with the knowledge and skills needed to succeed in education and careers after high school.

In the 2nd and 3rd iterations of this chapter we will discuss all aspects of TPEs and TPAs in detail.

Second Iteration

• •

This part explains what are the TPEs, TPAs and California Common Core State Standards.

Teacher Performance Expectations: _____

Teacher Performance Assessments: _____

California State Standards: _____

Coming to Terms over Teacher Performance
• •

Teacher Performance Expectations (TPE) are the descriptions of the "knowledge, skills, and abilities beginning teachers should have and be able to demonstrate. Teaching performance expectations describe teaching tasks that fall into six broad domains . . ."[1]

Teacher Performance Assessments (TPA) are "designed to measure the candidate's knowledge, skills and ability with relation to California's Teaching Performance Expectations (TPEs), including demonstrating his/her ability to appropriately instruct all K–12 students in the Student Academic Content Standards. Each of the three approved teaching performance assessment models requires a candidate to complete defined tasks relating to subject-specific pedagogy, designing and implementing instruction and student assessment, and a culminating teaching experience or event."[2]

---

[1]**Appendix A of the CalTPA Candidate Handbook** is covered by this Handbook's Copyright © 2008 by the California Commission on Teacher Credentialing http://www.ctc.ca.gov/educator-prep/TPA-files/CandidateHandbook-AppendixA-TPEs.pdf

[2]Teaching Performance Assessment (TPA) http://www.ctc.ca.gov/educator-prep/TPA.html

Teacher Performance Expectations and Teacher Performance Assessments in Action

On February 28, 1803, Congress gave President Thomas Jefferson the approval for a plan of discovery. The plan's mission was to explore the uncharted western region of the North American continent. Jefferson appropriately named the group the Corps of Discovery. That corps was led by Meriwether Lewis and William Clark.

In many ways California teachers in the ever more culturally and linguistically diverse classrooms from Oregon to the Mexican border must possess the same spirit of discovery as Lewis and Clark. Instead of traversing thousands of miles of uncharted territory with unexpected problems as did the Corps of Discovery, today's teachers deal with state standards, thousands of pages of content from textbooks and the Internet, appropriate methodological approaches to accommodate an array of learning styles, and various educational technologies, not to mention the many times unanticipated social, economic and political challenges that affect education in the Golden State.

Lewis and Clark began their journey with many expectations and ways to assess their progress. They also possessed a detailed action plan for their historic expedition that would insure the accomplishment of their goals. The purpose of this edition of *Writing Effective Lesson Plans* (WELP) is to merge the same elements—on the one hand, expectations and assessments (California Teaching Performance Expectations and California Teaching Performance Assessment) and the plan of action summed up in the 5-Star Approach: Lesson Description, Goals and Objectives, Materials and Tools, Procedure, and Reflective Assessment and Evaluation. It would provide a pathway to students' effective learning outcomes.

The TPA/TPE/WELP Matrix has been developed as a streamlined checklist to evaluate whether or not your lesson plan is meeting the Teaching Performance Assessments and Teaching Performance Expectations with the *Writing Effective Lesson Plans* 5-Star Approach. Before we introduce the matrix, however, let's consider the theoretical foundations behind the idea of expectations and assessments.

Expectations and Assessments

Expectations and assessments are the alpha and omega of teaching and learning. Setting expectations are critical because it relates to the student the notion of what should be accomplished. More than that, an expectation sets an articulated environment for both short range objectives and long range goals. High expectations point the way to successful outcomes just as low expectations become their own kind of self-fulfilling prophecy. Somebody said, "Nobody has risen to low expectations".

While in a conceptual sense expectations stand alone as a way to view task oriented prospects and personal potential, in the real world to know if an expectation has been met necessitates the notion of an assessment. Assessments answer the *what* and *how* of how an expectation is judged. In a lesson plan one can use many assessment tools to appraise a student's strengths and weaknesses. It is important, as we will see, not to confuse assessment and evaluation. Assessment is a dynamic and ongoing review of a student's academic development and social growth. Evaluation, on the other hand, is a static measurement via a test score, class ranking or final grade. Evaluation is precise, but has a finite quality to it as scores, rankings and grades are fundamentally immutable.

Teachers should consider how expectations, assessments and evaluations fit into a lesson plan. Make note of the idea that a lesson plan provides an open door to view how instruction is structured. The structure of a lesson plan sets a pathway for academic activities of a given class on a given day. While the lesson plan has a primary importance to the teacher who authored the particular arrangement of tasks, the lesson plan also can and/or should be viewed by substitute teachers, school administrators, parents—and yes, even the students themselves.

One 21st century innovation allows you to make your lesson plans available to all via your school web site on the Internet. With both your expectations and assessments functioning as bookends to your lesson plan available on the web, you will have provided access for all interested stakeholders whose primary interest is student success.

So, what are teacher performance expectations? Candidate teachers taking teacher preparation programs in California are required to demonstrate proficiency in the California Teaching Performance Expectations (TPEs) before obtaining their teaching credential. The California Commission on Teacher Credentialing (CCTC) developed TPEs as standards for the teaching profession to identify teacher qualifications. These thirteen (TPEs) are grouped into six Teaching Performance Domains. TPEs define what candidates should be able to demonstrate by the end of the teacher preparation program they take.

A complete version of the TPEs can be found on the CCTC website at **www.ctc.ca.gov**. Candidates taking a teacher preparation program must receive a Rubric Score of three on the Assessment and

Evaluation of Teaching Performance form at the end of their student teaching practice to successfully meet the TPE requirements and obtain the credit for student teaching experience. This is accomplished through four Tasks.

Teacher Performance Assessment

All 13 TPEs must be learned and practiced by the Teacher Preparation candidate, and objective, uniform assessments will be given to identify how candidates have learned to implement TPEs in the program. To assess this competency, Teaching Performance Assessment (TPA) is used as an assessment tool. Throughout the program, candidates will complete four TPA performance tasks to demonstrate their competency in all 13 TPE areas.

TPAs measures the candidate's knowledge, skills and ability with relation to (TPEs) via four different tasks that make up the (TPAs).

Each performance task measures various teaching performance expectations. Three of the four of the tasks are based on the needs of the ever more culturally and linguistically diverse students being taught. Task 4 analysis includes a lesson on video.

● WHAT'S THE PLAN?

Explain how TPEs and TPAs are related: (**Hint:** *Compare the TPEs and TPAs and you will see the correlation between them.*)

_____

_____

_____

_____

_____

_____

How this Book Responds to the TPEs

The purpose of this edition is to merge expectations and assessments as identifies in California Teaching Performance Expectations and California Teaching Performance Assessment, and the plan of action summed up in the 5-Star Approach: Lesson Description, Goals and Objectives, Materials and Tools, Procedure, and Reflective Assessment and Evaluation.

● **TABLE 1.1 TPE Domains in the WELP Book**

Domain A	Making Subject Matter Comprehensible to Students
	TPE 1 Specific Pedagogical Skills for Subject
	  Matter Instruction
		Ch. 5 Materials and Tools
		Ch. 6 Procedure
		Ch. 8 Knowledge Construction
		  and Skill Development
		Appendix

Domain B	Assessing Student Learning
	TPE 2 Monitoring Student Learning During
	  Instruction
	TPE 3 Interpretation and Use of Assessments
		Ch. 7 Reflective Assessment and
		  Evaluation

Domain C	Engaging and Supporting Students in Learning
	TPE 4 Making Content Accessible
	TPE 5 Student Engagement
	TPE 6 Developmentally Appropriate Teaching
	  Practices
	TPE 7 Teaching English Language Learners
		Ch. 5 Materials and Tools
		Ch. 6 Procedure
		Ch.12 Implementing the Plan
		Ch.13 Extending the Lesson Plan
		  Home

Domain D	Planning Instruction and Designing Learning
	  Experiences for Students
	TPE 8 Learning about Students
	TPE 9 Instructional Planning
		Ch. 2 (Lesson Plan) Structure
		  and Stages of Development
		Ch. 3 Lesson Description
		Ch. 10 Course and Lesson
		  Strategic and Tactical
		  Planning

Domain E	Creating and Maintaining an Effective Environment
	  for Students' Learning
	TPE 10 Instructional Time
	TPE 11 Social Environment
		Ch. 4 Goals and Objectives
		Ch. 11 Time Efficiency in
		  Teaching and Learning

Domain F	Developing as a Professional Educator TPE 12 Professional, Legal, and Ethical Obligations TPE 13 Professional Growth	Ch. 14 Teacher Professional Competence

● WHAT'S THE PLAN?

How are you going to demonstrate the knowledge of TPEs in lesson plans? (***Hint:*** *Use the Matrix.)*

_____

_____

_____

_____

_____

California Common Core State Standards

The California State Board of Education (SBE) adopted the new Common Core State Standards on August 2, 2010. It is a set of standards that would help prepare students with the knowledge and skills needed to succeed in education and careers after high school. The CCSS include standards for mathematics, English-language arts, and literacy in various content areas for students in kindergarten through grade twelve. More information about the development of the Common Core State Standards is available at the Common Core State Standards Initiative Web Site (http://www.cde.ca.gov/ci/cc/ccssfaqs2010.asp).

You can follow the development of the CCCSS at http://www.cde.ca.gov/ci/cc/. Needless to say, all teachers are expected to implement California Common Core State Standards in their lesson plans.

Your Turn—Practice Sheets

Please write which TPEs and how you will reflect on in your lesson plans. Explain how these TPEs can be assessed. How do you adhere to State Standards in your teaching?

I. TPEs: _____

_____

_____

_____

_____

II. TPAs: _____

_____

_____

_____

_____

III. State Standards: _____

_____

_____

_____

_____

_____

Third Iteration

• •

This part will add to your understanding of TPEs, TPAs and Common Core Standards.

Teaching Performance Expectations Summary[3]
• •

All 13 TPEs are grouped into six domains (Table 1.2.):

● **TABLE 1.2   TPE Domains**

Domain A	Making Subject Matter Comprehensible to Students TPE 1 Specific Pedagogical Skills for Subject Matter Instruction
Domain B	Assessing Student Learning TPE 2 Monitoring Student Learning During Instruction TPE 3 Interpretation and Use of Assessments
Domain C	Engaging and Supporting Students in Learning TPE 4 Making Content Accessible TPE 5 Student Engagement TPE 6 Developmentally Appropriate Teaching Practices TPE 7 Teaching English Language Learners
Domain D	Planning Instruction and Designing Learning Experiences for Students TPE 8 Learning about Students TPE 9 Instructional Planning
Domain E	Creating and Maintaining an Effective Environment for Students' Learning TPE 10 Instructional Time TPE 11 Social Environment
Domain F	Developing as a Professional Educator TPE 12 Professional, Legal, and Ethical Obligations TPE 13 Professional Growth

---

[3]CCTC website at **www.ctc.ca.gov**

Let's consider TPEs in detail.

A: MAKING SUBJECT MATTER COMPREHENSIBLE TO STUDENTS

TPE 1: Specific Pedagogical Skills for Subject Matter Instruction

Candidates demonstrate the ability to teach the state-adopted academic content standards and instruct in ways within a learning environment that develop skills in:

- **Reading and English Language Arts.** Deliver a comprehensive program that promotes learning to read and write, comprehension and composition, appreciation and analysis, as well as performance and enjoyment of the language arts.
- **Mathematics.** Teach basic computations, concepts, and symbols, problem solving through mathematical reasoning using concrete, verbal, symbolic, and graphic representation.
- **Science.** Explain and demonstrate scientific concepts, principles, investigation, and experimentation. Emphasize accuracy, precision, and estimation.
- **History and Social Science.** Teach basic analytical thinking skills through a variety of media. Develop insights into historical periods and cultures using social science concepts and themes. Provide multiple perspectives by using simulation, case studies, cultural artifacts, works of arts and literature, cooperative projects and student research.

B: ASSESSING STUDENT LEARNING

TPE 2: Monitoring Student Learning During Instruction

- Monitor student work at key points during instruction to check for adequate progress
- Pace instruction and re-teach content using assessment strategies such as questioning students and examining their work
- Anticipate, check for, and address common student misconceptions and misunderstandings

TPE 3: Interpretation and Use of Assessments

- Know how to familiarize students with, and administer assessment instruments
- Collect multiple sources of information to assess student learning
- Interpret assessment results
- Determine student progress and use results to plan instruction
- Teach students how to use self-assessment strategies. Provide time for practice
- Give students specific and timely feedback. Maintain accurate records of student achievement
- Work with families to help students achieve. Explain curriculum content and students' strengths and areas for growth

C: ENGAGING AND SUPPORTING STUDENTS IN LEARNING

TPE 4: Making Content Accessible

- Incorporate and sequence strategies, instructional materials and experiences that address state-adopted content standards
- Adjust lesson design to accommodate students' current level of achievement
- Vary strategies. Explain and reinforce content in multiple ways (presentation, manipulatives, models, the arts, diagrams, non-verbal communication, and technology)
- Develop students' academic language. Encourage their creativity and imagination

TPE 5: Student Engagement

- Clearly communicate learning objectives
- Use various instructional strategies and create relevant activities. Use community resources and student experiences
- Create stimulating discussions and challenge students by asking different types of questions using Bloom's taxonomy

- Monitor student progress. Encourage active/equitable participation. Re-engage off-task students using various instructional strategies

TPE 6: Developmentally Appropriate Teaching Practices

Establish expectations that are appropriate at distinct stages and adolescent development, such as:

- **In grades K–3:** Structure daily activities that allow for movement and attention span of young learners. Connect with their world. Use manipulatives and hands-on learning experiences. Teach and model norms of social interactions.
- **In grades 4–8:** Support students who lack basic skills. Teach from grade level texts. Extend concrete thinking; foster abstract reasoning and problem-solving skills. Help students develop effective learning strategies and assist them in time-management skills. Support new roles and responsibilities; facilitate group efforts and responsible behavior.
- **In grades 9–12:** Establish challenging academic expectations and clearly communicate these to students and families.

Understand adolescence and its challenges. Foster advanced abstract thinking and problem-solving skills. Connect curriculum to adult life. Encourage responsibility and individuality while acknowledging peer pressure.

TPE 7: Teaching English Learners

- Know and use effective ELD strategies leading to English literacy
- Differentiate instruction and select appropriate instructional materials and strategies based on individual language assessment data
- Collaborate with specialists and para-educators
- Develop students' academic knowledge and language in core subjects
- Use effective questioning strategies and model English constructions

D: PLANNING INSTRUCTION AND DESIGNING LEARNING EXPERIENCES FOR STUDENTS

TPE 8: Learning about Students

- Use knowledge of patterns of child and adolescent development to understand students
- Assess students' language abilities, content knowledge and skill, using both formal methods and interpersonal interactions
- Encourage, support and facilitate parent participation
- Understand how factors such as gender and health influence behavior and learning potential
- Use multiple means of assessment to identify students with special needs

TPE 9: Instructional Planning

- Plan comprehensive instruction based on state-adopted academic content standards
- Establish short and long term learning goals based on state and local standards as well as student current achievement levels
- Use a variety of explicit teaching methods
- Use experience and reflection to improve implementation of instructional strategies
- Sequence instruction appropriately, using effective strategies and instructional material
- Connect academic content with students' backgrounds, interests, and needs
- Differentiate instruction to accommodate students' needs
- Use support personnel to help students reach goals

E: CREATING AND MAINTAINING EFFECTIVE ENVIRONMENTS FOR STUDENT LEARNING

TPE 10: instructional Time

- Allocate instructional time to maximize student achievement
- Establish procedures for routine tasks and manage transitions efficiently

- Use reflection and consultation to adjust instructional time to optimize learning opportunities and outcomes

TPE 11: Social Environment

- Develop and maintain clear academic and behavioral expectations, effectively implementing a discipline plan
- Create a positive climate for learning by promoting student effort and engagement
- Establish rapport with students and their families through caring, respect, fairness and sensitivity
- Foster responsibility and independence in students
- Make necessary changes in the social environment to maximize academic achievement

F: DEVELOPING AS A PROFESSIONAL EDUCATOR

TPE 12: Professional, Legal and Ethical Obligations

- Take responsibility for student academic learning outcomes, ensuring that they are met
- Resist racism and acts of intolerance and maintain a non-hostile classroom environment
- Understand and implement state and federal law and school and district policies
- Understand and honor professional and legal obligations and model ethical behaviors

TPE 13: Professional Growth

- Evaluate their own teaching practices and subject matter knowledge and solicit feedback
- Improve their teaching practices by using reflection and feedback to formulate and prioritize goals

Effective teacher preparation of a lesson plan begins with the knowledge of Teaching Performance Expectations (TPEs). These expectations are the foundation of successful education and, specifically, of designing an effective lesson plan as they are providing an inherent rationale for the teaching and learning process. Lesson plan as a model of the future lesson should integrate all TPEs, especially 8–10. All teacher candidates in California must demonstrate competency in the TPEs.

Teaching Performance Assessment

TPAs measures the candidate's knowledge, skills and ability with relation to (TPEs) via four different tasks that make up the (TPAs).

Each performance task measures various teaching performance expectations. Three of the four of the tasks are based on the needs of the ever more culturally and linguistically diverse students being taught. Task 4 analysis includes a lesson on video.

Task 1: Subject Specific Pedagogy (understanding appropriate content, assessment and adaptation)

The Subject-Specific Pedagogy task contains four case studies which address subject-specific and developmentally-appropriate pedagogy, assessment practices, adaptation of content for English Learners, and adaptation of content for students with special needs.

Task 2: Designing Instruction (knowing the learner)

The Designing Instruction task requires demonstration of the ability to learn important details about a classroom of students, an English learner, and a student who presents a difficult instructional challenge.

Task 3: Assessing Learning (planning to reach goals in standards-based appropriate assessment)

The Assessing Learning task requires demonstration of the ability to select a unit of study, identify related learning goals, and plan standards-based, developmentally-appropriate student assessment activities for a group of students.

Task 4: Culminating Teaching Experience (implementing plan)

The Culminating Teaching Experience task requires demonstration of the ability to design a standards-based lesson for a class of students, implement that lesson while making appropriate use of class time and instructional resources, meeting the different needs of individuals within the class, and managing instruction and student interaction.

When you follow the 5-Star Approach in writing your lesson plan you will already be fulfilling the guidelines that make up what is called the Teaching Performance Assessment (TPA).

● WHAT'S THE PLAN?

Identify the six TPE domains:

1. _____

2. _____

3. _____

4. _____

5. _____

6. _____

TPA Tasks

Tasks are assignments given to students during their program which will serve as assessment items for TPA. They embrace four topics:

1. Subject Specific Pedagogy
2. Designing Instruction
3. Assessing Learning
4. Culminating Teaching Experience

Each of the topics is represented in several case studies.

Task 1: Subject Specific Pedagogy

The Subject-Specific Pedagogy task contains four case studies which address subject-specific and developmentally-appropriate pedagogy, assessment practices, adaptation of content for English Learners, and adaptation of content for students with special needs. In this task, candidates will respond in writing to each of the four case studies.

This task assesses the candidate's ability to understand how information about a class is used to:

- Prepare instruction for particular subjects and content areas
- Develop and adapt student assessment plans based on the content

Performance Context

The candidate is given four case studies of specific classes and learners. The candidate develops:

Case Study 1: Teaching methods and lesson plans focused on the content

Case Study 2: Analyses and adaptations of assessment plans focused on the content

Case Study 3: Adaptations of the lesson plans for English learners

Case Study 4: Adaptations of the lesson plans for students with special needs

In addition, candidates provide written reflections on their responses to the case studies. TPEs addressed within this task: 1, 2, 4, 6, and 7.

This is the only CalTPA task in which the candidate does not work with K–12 students.

Task 2: Designing Instruction

The Designing Instruction task requires demonstration of the ability to learn important details about a classroom of students, an English learner, and a student who presents a difficult instructional challenge. In this task candidates will plan instruction that is shaped by and addresses those student characteristics and demonstrate the candidate's ability to connect learning about students to instructional planning.

This task assesses the candidate's ability to identify the links between students' characteristics and their learning needs, and to:

- Plan instruction for an actual class of K–12 students, including developing and adapting instruction for English learners and for students with other instructional challenges

- Reflect on the connections between student characteristics and instructional planning

Performance Context

The candidate is given a five-step set of prompts:

> **Step 1:** Selecting the content to be taught and learning about the students
>
> **Step 2:** Learning about two focus students: an English learner and a student with a different instructional challenge
>
> **Step 3:** Planning academic instruction for the whole class
>
> **Step 4:** Adapting academic instruction for the two focus students
>
> **Step 5:** Reflecting on what has been learned through the task

TPEs addressed within this task: 1, 4, 6, 7, 8, 9, and 13.
This task is completed with K–12 students.

Task 3: Assessing Learning

Assessing Learning task requires demonstration of the ability to select a unit of study, identify related learning goals, and plan standards-based, developmentally appropriate student assessment activities for a group of students. In this task candidates will demonstrate the ability to assess student learning and diagnose student needs based on student responses to the assessment activity, and show how to apply this information to future planning for these students.

Candidates will also demonstrate the ability to make assessment adaptations for two focus students: an English learner and a student with identified special needs.

This task assesses the candidate's ability to assess students' learning. The candidate:

- Plans student assessment activities based on the learning goals
- Administers student assessments to evaluate student learning
- Adapts the assessments for English learners and for students with other instructional challenges
- Analyzes and uses assessment results to plan instruction
- Reflects on assessment implementation and the connection to student learning

Performance Context

The candidate is given a five-step set of prompts:

Step 1: Selecting the assessment content and planning for the assessment

Step 2: Learning about the whole class and two focus students: an English learner and student with an identified special need

Step 3: Adapting the assessment for the two focus students

Step 4: Analyzing assessment evidence of student academic learning

Step 5: Reflecting on what has been learned through the task

TPEs addressed within this task: 3, 6, 7, 8, 9, and 13
This task is completed with K–12 students.

Task 4: Culminating Teaching Experience

The Culminating Teaching Experience task requires demonstration of the ability to design a standards-based lesson for a class of students, implement that lesson while making appropriate use of class time and instructional resources, meeting the different needs of individuals within the class, and managing instruction and student interaction. In this task candidates will demonstrate the ability to assess student learning related to the lesson, and analyze the overall strengths and weaknesses of the lesson.

Candidates will be required to obtain parent permission to video-tape students in their assigned classroom and verification must be submitted to TaskStream. The permission slips may be obtained in TaskStream. We recommend candidates keep the signed permission slips for their records. Candidates are responsible for video recording their lesson.

This task assesses the candidate's ability to integrate the strands of the previous three tasks. The candidate:

- Learns about students, and plans student instruction and assessment activities based on the learning goals adapts the plans and assessments for English learners and for students with other instructional challenges
- Teaches the lesson and administers the assessments
- Analyzes and uses instruction and assessment results to plan further instruction

- Reflects on the lesson, the classroom instruction, the learning results, and on his/her effectiveness as a teacher

Performance Context

The candidate is given a six-step set of prompts:

> **Step 1:** Learning about the whole class and two focus students: an English learner and a student with a different instructional challenge
>
> **Step 2:** Planning academic instruction for the whole class
>
> **Step 3:** Adapting the lesson for the two focus students
>
> **Step 4:** Teaching and video recording the lesson
>
> **Step 5:** Analyzing the lesson and the evidence of student academic learning
>
> **Step 6:** Reflecting on what has been learned through the task

TPEs Addressed Within This Task: 1, 2, 3, 4, 5, 6, 7, 8, 9, 10, 11, and 13

This task is completed with K–12 students.

These tasks are summed up in five basic actions you need to demonstrate:

- Find out information about a given class and about specific focus students within the class such as an English learner or a student with identified special needs
- Plan appropriate subject-specific instruction for all students in alignment with state-adopted K–12 student academic content standards and/or frameworks
- Implement the instruction according to the lesson plans you have developed, and reflect upon the outcomes of that instruction, including evidence of student learning
- Design and implement assessment activities appropriate to the lesson and to the learners, and use the assessment results to inform the next round of lesson planning
- Reflect upon your own professional growth as a member of the teaching profession[4]

---

[4]CalTPA Candidate Handbook (2008), Sacramento: California Commission on Teacher Credentialing.

TPA Tasks and Corresponding chapters in WELP

Each chapter in this book connects to TPA and its tasks.

● **TABLE 1.3   TPA Tasks and WELP**

Task	WELP Chapters
Subject Specific Pedagogy	Ch. 8 Knowledge Construction and Skill Development Ch. 5 Materials and Tools Ch. 6 Procedure Appendix
Designing Instruction	Ch. 2 (Lesson Plan) Structure and Stages of Development Ch. 3 Lesson Description Ch. 4 Goals and Objectives Ch. 11 Time Efficiency in Teaching and Learning Ch. 10 Course and Lesson Strategic and Tactical Planning
Assessing Learning	Ch. 7 Reflective Assessment and Evaluation
Culminating Teaching Experience	Ch. 6 Procedure Ch.12 Implementing the Plan Ch.13 Extending the Lesson Plan Home and teaching the designed lesson

TPE and WELP Matrix

The matrix presented below connects all 13 TPEs and WELP chapters.

● **TABLE 1.4   Matrix for TPE and WELP Materials**

TPE	What to Do and Where to find the Related Material
1. Specific Pedagogical Skills for Subject Matter Instruction	To promote learning to read and write, basic mathematics and science concepts and skills, and develop analytical thinking skills and insights in history and social sciences, use organizing, structuring and modeling guidelines in Ch. 8. Apply strategies, activities and tools described in Ch. 5 and 6.
2. Monitoring Student Learning During Instruction	Monitor student work using assessment techniques described in Ch. 7 and pace it applying time evaluation strategies from Ch. 11.
3. Interpretation and Use of Assessments	Integrate assessment and evaluation in your lessons and teach students self-assessment using material of Ch. 7.

4. Making Content Accessible	Incorporate and sequence strategies, instructional materials and experiences; adjust lessons and use multiple presentation media based on material in Ch. 5, 6, 12 and 13.
5. Student Engagement	Clearly communicate learning objectives using Ch. 3 and 4. Use various instructional strategies and create relevant activities using Ch. 6 and 12. Use community resources and student experiences referring to Ch. 13.
6. Developmentally Appropriate Teaching Practices	Establish expectations that are appropriate at distinct stages and adolescent development using material from Ch. 3.
7. Teaching English Learners	Differentiate instruction and select appropriate instructional materials and strategies using Ch. 12 and 6.
8. Learning about Students	Incorporate knowledge of your students into teaching using materials from Ch. 3, 7 and 13.
9. Instructional Planning	Plan comprehensive instruction based on Ch. 2, 4, 7, 10 and 12.
10. Instructional Time	Allocate instructional time and plan effectively using Ch. 11 and 3.
11. Social Environment	Develop and maintain clear academic and behavioral expectations, create a positive climate for learning, establish rapport with students and their families using Ch. 4, 6, 12 and 13.
12. Professional, Legal and Ethical Obligations	Take responsibility for student academic learning outcomes, understand and implement state and federal law and school and district policies using Ch. 12.
13. Professional Growth	Reflect on, assess and improve instructional practices and own competencies in subject matter and teaching methodology Ch. 14.

● WHAT'S THE PLAN?

How are you going to demonstrate the knowledge of TPEs in lesson plans? (**Hint:** Use the Matrix.)

_____

_____

_____

_____

_____

California Common Core State Standards

California Common Core State K–12 Standards are:

- Aligned with college and work expectations;
- Include rigorous content *and* application of knowledge through high-order skills;
- Build upon strengths and lessons of current state standards;
- Informed by top-performing countries, so that all students are prepared to succeed in our global economy and society; and,
- Evidence and/or research-based.

They will become mandatory in all schools starting 2014.
An example of the CCCSS:

College and Career Readiness Anchor Standards for Reading

The grades 6–12 standards on the following pages define what students should understand and be able to do by the end of each grade. They correspond to the College and Career Readiness (CCR) anchor standards below by number.

The CCR and grade-specific standards are necessary complements—the former providing broad standards, the latter providing additional specificity—that together define the skills and understandings that all students must demonstrate.

Key Ideas and Details

1. Read closely to determine what the text says explicitly and to make logical inferences from it; cite specific textual evidence when writing or speaking to support conclusions drawn from the text.
2. Determine central ideas or themes of a text and analyze their development; summarize the key supporting details and ideas.
3. Analyze how and why individuals, events, and ideas develop and interact over the course of a text.

Craft and Structure

4. Interpret words and phrases as they are used in a text, including determining technical, connotative, and figurative meanings, and analyze how specific word choices shape meaning or tone.

5. Analyze the structure of texts, including how specific sentences, paragraphs, and larger portions of the text (e.g., a section, chapter, scene, or stanza) relate to each other and the whole.

6. Assess how point of view or purpose shapes the content and style of a text.

Integration of Knowledge and Ideas

7. Integrate and evaluate content presented in diverse formats and media, including visually and quantitatively, as well as in words.

8. Delineate and evaluate the argument and specific claims in a text, including the validity of the reasoning as well as the relevance and sufficiency of the evidence.

9. Analyze how two or more texts address similar themes or topics in order to build knowledge or to compare the approaches the authors take.

Range of Reading and Level of Text Complexity

10. Read and comprehend complex literary and informational texts independently and proficiently

http://www.corestandards.org/assets/CCSSI_ELA%20Standards.pdf
   You can follow the development of the CCCSS at http://www.cde .ca.gov/ci/cc/
   Needless to say, all teachers are expected to implement California Common Core State Standards in their lesson plans.

Now that you have an understanding of what TPEs are and how you are going to be assessed on the application of TPEs using TPAs in your lesson plan and teaching, we will clarify what a lesson plan is, what are its structure and sequence of its components, and how to design it effectively.

CHAPTER 2

Lesson Plan Structure and Stages of Development

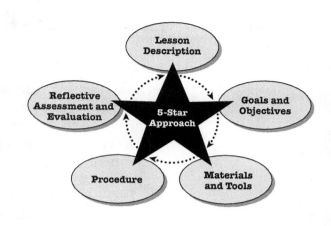

First Iteration

> *"Planning is bringing the future into the present so that you can do something about it now"* (Alan Lakein).

Before the first students come through the classroom door, the teacher must be prepared to begin the learning process based on a plan of action. Teaching actually consists of planned behaviors intended to induce learning (Michael Moore). This chapter will define a lesson plan, examine the rationale for planning, indicate the stages of lesson plan development, and describe the sequencing of lesson components. A well-thought out lesson plan gives the teacher a sense of direction and may well foster a feeling of confidence and enthusiasm in implementing instruction thereby setting an atmosphere for learning.

A lesson plan is *a **model of specially selected and consistently organized learning events within a standard time period of a formal instructional process***. Constructed by a teacher, it determines the structure and sequence of the teaching and learning activities to be performed during that period. Both the teacher and students will perform these planned activities intended to achieve the learning goals and specific objectives of the lesson. The plan helps create the necessary circumstances and conditions for students' productive learning, however it does not and should not restrict activities contributing to the lesson's success that come up during the procedure.

A lesson plan is a projection of a real lesson, a structure filled with concrete processes, assignments and learning tools. Moreover, it usually includes everything necessary for the lesson implementation, such as: teaching/learning materials, activity banks, visuals, handouts, and technological applications. So, a lesson plan is actually a model of the lesson to be taught in the future.

A typical lesson plan structure includes the following five components:

1. Lesson Description
2. Goals and objectives
3. Materials and tools
4. Procedures
5. Assessment and evaluation

Lesson procedure is the implementation of a lesson plan; it is, in fact, a projection of the lesson plan structure on the temporal axis of the actual lesson. It includes five major steps:

1. Introduction
2. Content presentation
3. Activities
4. Assessment and evaluation
5. Closure

The lesson plan structure and its implementation in five steps are the most important concepts of effective lesson planning. In the next chapters we will discuss each of the lesson plan components in detail so you could design the plan that meets state standards, student needs and your expectations.

Lesson Plan

Description
Goal, objectives and learning outcomes
Tools and materials
Procedure
Assessment and evaluation
Closure

In the 2nd and 3rd iterations of this chapter we will explain how to structure an effective lesson plan.

Second Iteration

This chapter will examine the lesson plan structure and stages of development. You will identify what the plan consists of, and how to organize teaching and learning events in a lesson.

Lesson Plan

Description _____

Goal, objectives and learning outcomes _____

Tools and materials _____

Procedure _____

    Introduction _____

    Content presentation _____

    Student activities _____

Assessment and evaluation tools and techniques _____

    Assessment and evaluation _____

Closure _____

Coming to Terms Over Defining and Designing a Plan

A **plan** is a systematic means to reach an end. Quality teaching, like any other occupation, requires rational and sound planning, organization and management. One of the prerequisites for achieving this goal is the teacher's competency in lesson plan development. Therefore planning becomes an important part of every practitioner's professional development.

Lesson planning is essential in almost any aspect of daily classroom life. Good lesson plans are the foundation of successful student learning, accurate assessment, and effective classroom management. Every teacher, at some point, needs clear guidelines for designing and implementing quality lessons. Lesson plan development followed by instructional practice and reflective assessment is a key to successful teaching. A well-structured plan might, in a sense, mirror a rational approach due to its clear and concise format. Nevertheless, the authors accept a constructivist view of learning in which the sum and substance of the learning experience is ultimately controlled by the learner.

Constructivism is based on the notion of building up one's own knowledge via the interaction between prior knowledge and new knowledge, and integration of the new knowledge in the interactions between a learner and peers and the instructor. It is an ongoing process of gathering new knowledge and actively engaging, questioning, problem solving, and collaborating with others to build new meanings. Because we traditionally learn in a social environment we also collaboratively build a common knowledge that will eventually be interiorized by each member of the learning community individually. Lesson planning is about designing learner engagement in activities that provide for knowledge construction and skill development.

So, What Is a Lesson Plan?

When you first approach the lesson plan it is important to understand a Gestalt (structure or pattern) of the model. You may well find that the **5-Star Lesson Plan** presents a convenient way to conceptualize an overview of a fairly detailed process that may evolve in various shapes.

A **lesson plan** is *a model of organized learning events within a standard time period of a formal instructional process*. Constructed by a teacher, it determines the structure and sequence of the teaching and learning activities to be performed during that period. Both the teacher and students will perform these planned activities intended to achieve the learning goals and specific objectives of the lesson. Improvisation on the part of the teacher and students might be useful and even necessary as long as it aligns with the goals and objectives and enhances the learning outcomes. It is good to remember, however, that if you want to improvise, your quality preparation will make those improvisations successful.

A lesson plan is a projection of a real lesson, a structure filled with concrete processes, assignments and learning tools. Moreover, it usually includes everything necessary for the lesson implementation, such as: teaching/learning materials, activity banks, visuals, handouts, and technological applications. So, a lesson plan is actually a model of the lesson to be taught in the future.

A lesson plan is a blueprint on which to construct a learning process made up of clearly stated goals and objectives which research has shown (Gronlund 2000) enhances student outcomes. Accordingly, a clear and well-organized structure used to obtain and process information promotes superior retention as compared to a less organized information model (Fuchs et al. 1997). Communicating *in advance* via a lesson plan what the students are to achieve permits a teacher to devise reflective assessments and evaluations to measure progress.

The plan helps create the necessary circumstances and conditions for students' productive learning, however it does not and should not restrict activities contributing to the lesson's success that come up during the procedure. Improvisation on the part of the teacher and students might be useful and even necessary as long as it aligns with the goals and objectives and enhances the learning outcomes. It is good to remember, however, that if you want to improvise, your quality preparation will make those improvisations successful.

Finally, a lesson plan is a tool that moves from theory to practice (effective lesson plans are based on the most up-to-date educational research) by carrying out a methodological approach structured enough to ensure clear and concise direction, yet flexible enough to provide for differentiation to meet the needs of every student.

Stages of Lesson Plan Development

Lesson planning is a specific teacher's activity focused on designing and developing a practical model and procedure for future lessons. There are four main areas of planning:

1. Preparation
2. Development
3. Implementation
4. Rationale and reflection

PREPARATION

The first question you have to consider when starting your lesson plan is *Who* is to be taught? For instance:

- Identify your students, their abilities, background, and challenges.
- Select the relevant content and strategies responsive to the learner's needs by investigating his or her prior knowledge and individual characteristics (i.e. their "personal and cultural toolbox.") and recognize their learning needs so as to achieve the desired outcomes.
- Think of specific strategies and activities which will be most effective for student particular learning styles and which engage them in learning so the desired learning outcomes are achieved.

Thus, through knowing your students you will prepare for differentiating, adapting and accommodating your teaching to their individual levels, and use effective modification strategies.

● WHAT'S THE PLAN?

Identify your student's abilities, background and behavioral characteristics:

_____

_____

_____

Identify the needs of English Learners:

_____

_____

_____

Identify the needs of special education students:

_____

_____

_____

Identify the needs of high achieving students:

_____

_____

_____

Identify the most essential needs of your whole class:

_____

_____

_____

Design differentiating, adapting and accommodating strategies for students with exceptionalities:

_____

_____

_____

DEVELOPMENT

Now you identify the subject area and content—*What* is to be taught? For instance:

- Lesson's instructional goals
- Specific learning objectives
- State standards
- Concepts
- Content
- Life skills

● WHAT'S THE PLAN?

As you approach the stage of developing a lesson plan, think of the difference between teaching concepts and content. (***Hint:*** *Note the distinction between teaching concrete and abstract subject matter.*)

_____

_____

IMPLEMENTATION OF THE PLAN

As we know, how you teach determines what your students will learn. *How* do you usually teach students? What works best in your classrooms? For instance, which methodological approaches do you apply?

- Direct instruction
- Collaborative learning activities (group or team work)
- Self-directed learning
- Peer tutoring

What instructional tools and strategies do you use?

- Lesson structure and design
- Instructional materials and technology applications
- Instructional procedures and learning activities
- Reflective evaluation and assessment tools and techniques

● WHAT'S THE PLAN?

How are you going to teach your content area topic? (**Hint:** *lecturing a class from the textbook, offering students to independently search for the information on the topic on the internet, dividing them into small groups and giving them handouts asking to prepare presentations for the class, or other teaching strategies.*)

_____

_____

_____

_____

_____

RATIONALE AND REFLECTION

The fourth and final area of planning consists of two R's, a rationale and reflection. A **rationale** is a justification of your planning decisions, so to say a foundation of your plan. This is where you analyze the strengths and weaknesses of your lesson plan before implementing. It helps ensure its integrity and consistency and determine its potential for achieving the lesson's goal, objectives and outcomes. For instance, you can ask yourself:

- Does my plan adequately prepare all students for life challenges?
- Are the goals and objectives in line with the standards?
- Do I have the needed materials and tools to effectively carry out the lesson plan?
- Are the activities in my procedures geared to accommodate different learning styles?
- Am I specifically assessing and evaluating knowledge and/or skills that relate to the aforementioned goals and objectives?
- Have I designed a lesson that is culturally responsive?

● WHAT'S THE PLAN?

Review the lesson plan you have written and provide a rationale for each component and for the whole plan. Analyze it from the point of view of its effectiveness addressing the following questions:

Have I set the goal, objectives and learning outcomes correctly?

_____

_____

Will the procedure ensure successful accomplishment of the lesson's goal, objectives and learning outcomes?

_____

_____

Will the introduction to the lesson prepare students for effective learning and bridge the new material to the previously learned?

_____

_____

Are student activities organized so students will effectively construct knowledge and develop specified skills?

_____

_____

Will my assessment and evaluation help students improve their learning outcomes?

_____

_____

Will the homework provide the necessary extension of classroom learning and connect it to real life?

_____

_____

Does anybody need additional help? Have I made accommodations for ELs and students with special needs?

_____

_____

Who needs enrichment or higher level work?

_____

_____

Reflection is a critical self-assessment procedure done after the lesson has been taught. Here are the questions you might want to address:

- Have I achieved the planned goals and objectives?
- Did student learning outcomes meet the expectations?
- Have my students been active, engaged, and enjoyed the class?
- What worked and what did not, and how could I have done better?

Based on the reflection you can write a list of the things you noticed in your teaching that need improvement and use it when writing your next plan.

● WHAT'S THE PLAN?

Collect student learning data from the lesson you have taught to determine the following:

What went well? _____

_____

What needs to be changed? _____

_____

Were learning outcomes met? _____

_____

_____

What activities will I add, change, modify next time?_____

_____

_____

What can I do to improve my teaching and student learning in the future?

_____

_____

Structuring a Lesson Plan

All effective lesson plans have a structure. Typically, lesson plans follow this structure in writing. We call this lesson plan the **5-Star Lesson Plan** (Serdyukov & Ryan 2008) (Fig. 2.1).

● **FIGURE 2.1   The 5-Star Lesson Plan**

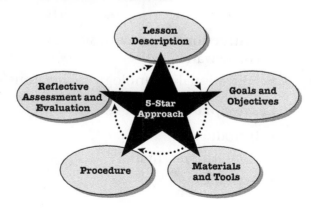

Actually, within this generic structure the teacher selects the most useful lesson plan model that responds best to students' learning styles and prior knowledge. An example of this typical structure elaboration is demonstrated in the National University Lesson Plan Template (Appendix 1). Correspondingly, the teacher strives to present the most enriched curriculum using the widest variety of methodological approaches.

Each lesson plan includes the following structural components:

1. *A plan's description*

   - The date
   - Subject area
   - Lesson's topic
   - Class grade (level)
   - Student body (individual characteristics)

   According to students' developmental level, the teacher considers differentiation, adaptation and accommodation of the lesson to their individual levels. Diverse populations considered:

   - English language learners (ELL)
   - Special education students
   - High achieving students

2. *General goals, specific objectives and learning outcomes*

   - A goal
   - Objectives
   - Learning outcomes
   - Academic and culturally relevant content standards

3. *Teacher's materials and tools*

   - Instructional resources, such as texts, handouts, visuals and courseware
   - Educational technology applications

4. *Lesson procedure (Fig. 2.2)*

   - Introduction
   - Content presentation
   - Activities

● **FIGURE 2.2   Lesson Plan Structure**

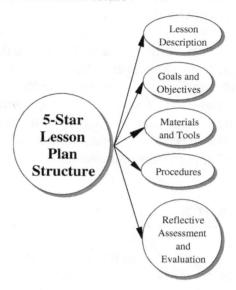

- Assessment and evaluation
- Homework assignment
- Closure

5. *Reflective assessment and evaluation*

- Assessment of students' performance
- Evaluation (tests, quizzes and essays)
- Lesson plan rationale and lesson's implementation reflection

A Generic Lesson Plan

A generic lesson plan is a typical structure accepted for designing a lesson. It consists of five parts:

1. Description
2. Goals, objectives and outcomes
3. Learning materials and tools
4. Lesson procedure
5. Assessment and evaluation

The **description** contains all the essential information about the lesson plan: the date of the lesson, subject area, topic, grade, goals and objectives, standards, and rationale. It may also include the teacher's name and general class characteristics, such as the number of students, their developmental level, the number of ELLs, their ESL proficiency, and special education students' needs.

Note: NU Template suggests identifying Grade Level K–12 Academic Content here, and to include standard(s), rationale, focus learner, and behavior expectations. State standards, in our opinion, better align with lesson goal, objectives and outcomes.

● WHAT'S THE PLAN?

What is the rationale for teaching what you plan and using instructional strategies, tools and materials?

_____

_____

_____

_____

What lesson plan adaptations might you employ depending on your audience?

_____

_____

_____

_____

Setting the **goals, objectives** and defining the learning **outcomes** occurs when the rationale for the lesson is given, the content standards identified and the explanation of why the lesson is important for the learner is clear. In a sense, the lesson plan starts with a statement of goals and objectives, and permeates through all the activities until lesson outcomes are achieved.

It is also useful to point out interdisciplinary connections and academic content standards (state approved standards), and explain to students how this lesson fits into their curriculum. In every lesson, the teacher should always make reference to what is being learned, why it is important for the student, and how it relates to other learning and their own lives. Therefore, the learner should be aware of the relevance of a specific knowledge, skill or activity. John Dewey (Dewey 1938) once remarked that learning is not merely acquiring information, but making that learning relevant to our everyday life.

● WHAT'S THE PLAN?

When stating the lesson goal, objectives and outcomes, ask the following questions:

What will students be able to do as a result of this lesson?

_____

_____

_____

How will you measure the mastery of the outcomes?

_____

_____

_____

Note: *It is important to make students aware of the lesson goal, objectives and planned outcomes in the beginning of the lesson. Then their learning will be more relevant and thus more effective.*

The **materials and tools** are the instructional resources and technological hardware and software the teacher needs in order to present, implement, and measure the efficacy of a given lesson plan. Video and multimedia, in addition to printed text and images, can be very effective presentation tools. The lesson plan normally includes a list of materials and other teaching and learning resources, as well as technology applications.

For example, teaching and learning materials, books, visuals, (charts, pictures, slides, posters), manipulatives and realia make up some of your options. Also critical to the contemporary classroom is educational technology in terms of hardware (overhead and LCD projectors, computers, DVD players) and courseware (overhead transparencies with images or text, videos and computer software—educational programs and games, and PowerPoint slides). You have to select among the available tools those that will best serve your lesson objectives. Recall: How you present new information will affect how students will understand and retain it.

Note: NU Template calls this component 'Resources' which include materials needed for this lesson accounting for varying degrees of skill level. It is necessary to note, however, that this component should also include, besides the materials, instructional tools.

● WHAT'S THE PLAN?

What instructional tools do you use to make your presentation of new material more effective and motivational? (***Hint:*** *Think of visuals, projectors, video, multimedia, and PowerPoint.*)

_____

_____

_____

What instructional tools and materials will you use for particular activities?

_____

_____

_____

Lesson procedure is the implementation of a lesson plan; it is, in fact, a projection of the lesson plan structure on the temporal axis of the actual lesson. The **procedure** usually includes five steps:

- Introduction
- New material presentation
- Student activities
- Assessment and evaluation
- Closure

Introduction is the initial part or phase of the lesson intended to prepare students for learning by warming up, general conversation, reviewing the previous lesson's key points, and finding out what prior knowledge the students may have (bridging). It may also include checking homework.

New material presentation is the phase where the fresh information is introduced by the teacher in the form of an expository lecture or a narrative, or by reading from a text. Often the teacher uses various visuals germane to the area of study. Presentation may be enhanced by educational technology applications, such as slides, video clips, multimedia shows and PowerPoint demonstrations.

Presentations can at times be made by students if they have been given a home assignment to search for new information or develop a project and present it in the class. The presentation phase is extremely important as is sets the model from which the students will learn.

Student activities include various activities and assignments that can be done individually or collaboratively, among which are: Q&A, exercises, case studies, problem-solving, role playing, discussions, presentations, and demonstrations. These activities may be of at least two levels of complexity: *basic* (guided exercises) and *advanced* (independent practice).

The difference between these levels is as follows: basic activities are to be accomplished according to patterns or simple models, with little flexibility in their implementation and guided by the teacher. This is done on purpose because the objective here is to develop initial skills, simulating or imitating a certain sample and using particular predetermined knowledge. In teaching ESL, for instance, these activities include various language exercises, such as drills, close testing, substitution, multiple choice, and simple communicative activities, such as simulation and role playing.

Advanced activities, on the other hand, are less controlled (some teacher guidance may be helpful, however), and allow for more freedom and flexibility in their implementation. Students are not limited in their performance except by the task, topic, setting and purpose of the particular activity. Examples of practice are dramatization, real-life simulations, games and project development.

An important aspect of all activities is the application of new material and skills in real-life or simulated situations, whether it is in the classroom, on the computer, with homework or in community service.

Note: NU Template reflects the same generic structure and singles out three types of the learning activities:

1. *Explicit Teacher Instruction—(Explain, Model, Demonstrate, Check for Understanding) which is actually New Material Presentation*

2. *Guided Practice/Collaborative Practice (Check for understanding and provide feedback and re-teaching.)*

3. *Independent Practice: (Provide practice that supports the learning outcome. **Note:** Independent activities are assigned assuming that students understand the concept well enough to work on their own.)*

The latter two activities correspond to the same activities identified in the generic lesson plan, whereas teacher presentation of the new materials may constitute a separate component.

Homework is an assignment to be done at home. Assigning homework is a process that entails giving and explaining the assignments to be done at home. These assignments serve as extension activities to reinforce or broaden the content covered and competencies developed. They literally extend the school day. What is important about homework is that students are given creative and useful assignments that are focused not only on providing retention but also on developing specific knowledge and skills.

Compare the two assignments:

Assignment One:

"Read the text, do exercises 35 and 37."

Assignment Two:

"In the text, find out what the hero was doing on a particular day, try to explain his acts and suggest options and alternative ways to achieve the purpose."

Clearly, the second assignment requires a creative approach that would include higher order critical thinking skills, whereas assignment one is just a formal task.

● WHAT'S THE PLAN?

Now, write an assignment for a class in the style and with the substance of Assignment Two:

_____

_____

_____

_____

_____

We judge of the efficacy of our teaching and student learning by reflective **assessment and evaluation** of what has been learned. Assessment can be conducted in the form of questions or dialogue between the teacher and the student to determine that student's strengths and weaknesses. Evaluation, which takes the form of a score, grade or ranking, can be conducted by a written test, examination or a quiz. Remember, checking for understanding is just an initial step in assessing your student's perception and progress.

Both assessment and evaluation can also be integrated in the activities phase when the teacher judges students' performance. Genuine assessments are ongoing and informal, as the teacher is continuously assessing the class and each individual student's performance and progress. This requires a teacher to possess both a competent judgment and a caring attitude.

A part of assessment and evaluation is checking up on homework. Students present their assigned out-of-class work, either by making oral presentations, or by turning in written work. It is important that the students realize that, "We don't do disposable work." Because corrected homework is never "a throw away exercise", after homework has been corrected, and if need be, revised to be brought up to standard, it is should be of high enough quality to be posted on a classroom bulletin board. A classroom full of high quality student work provides a model that demonstrably meets a high standard. When the bulletin boards are full, old work is taken down and put in a portfolio. This honors the work, and provides a qualitative record for teachers, students, parents and administrators.

The teacher reaches closure when the lesson plan has been completed. **Closure**, then, is a phase that incorporates the reflective review of the lesson and the summary of the lesson's key points. It also includes a general appraisal (assessment and evaluation) of the students' work and a short preview of the lesson to come.

● WHAT'S THE PLAN?

How is assessment different from evaluation in your opinion?

_____

_____

What assessment and evaluation techniques are you going to use in your lesson?

_____

_____

_____

Your Turn—Practice Sheets

Please construct a lesson plan for your future lesson by filling out this template.

1. DESCRIPTION

Date: _____

Subject: _____

_____

Topic: _____

_____

Grade: _____

2. GOALS, OBJECTIVES AND OUTCOMES

Goal: _____

_____

_____

Objectives: _____

_____

_____

Learning outcomes: _____

_____

_____

Standards: _____

_____

_____

Accommodations for EL and special education students: _____

_____

_____

Basic vocabulary: _____

_____

_____

Rationale: _____

_____

_____

3. MATERIALS AND TOOLS

Texts: _____

_____

Visuals: _____

_____

Technologies: _____

_____

Handouts: _____

_____

Rationale: _____

_____

4. PROCEDURE

Introduction (. . . min.): _____

_____

_____

Teacher presentation (. . . min.): _____

_____

_____

Class activities (. . . min.): _____
_____
_____
_____

Homework (. . . min.): _____
_____
_____
_____

Closure (. . . min.): _____
_____
_____
_____

Rationale: _____
_____
_____
_____

5. ASSESSMENT AND/OR EVALUATION

Teacher-student conferences: _____
_____
_____

Testing: _____
_____
_____

Rationale: _____
_____
_____

Third Iteration

* *

This iteration will discuss other approaches to lesson planning.

Lesson Plan Designs

There are different ways to design a lesson plan: a narrative, a "bullet format," a block scheme and an algorithm (a step-by-step procedure that often involves repetition).

A narrative is convenient for a beginning teacher who may prefer to have everything written out. It looks like a script of a play where everything is written: what the teacher does and says, and what the students are supposed to do.

Example: "In the beginning of the lesson, I will ask students some questions in order to identify what they know about a topic. Then I will read the text during which I will explain to them . . . ." This format may seem convenient but it does not present an explicit structure to the lesson and will be difficult to follow.

A bullet format lists the steps of the lesson, such as "read the text," "ask students questions," "give students assignment," or "have students write their problem solution on the board."

Example:

1. Ask questions on the previous lesson.
2. Read the text.
3. Explain the new words.
4. Organize a small group discussion.

This is the most frequently used format.

A block scheme presents a lesson structure in a graphic form, thus allowing the teacher to see all the activities to be performed in the lesson in a predetermined sequence and interrelation. In this format, the lesson plan can be presented as a modular structure (Fig. 2.3). Each module corresponds to a specific part or phase of the lesson with particular objectives, content, and activities, (e.g. new material presentation, or classroom activities aimed at developing particular skills). A typical lesson plan structure includes the following five components:

● **FIGURE 2.3   Lesson Plan Structure**

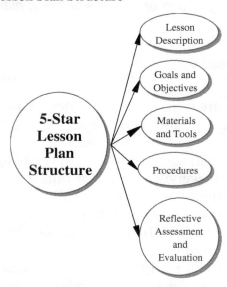

Putting it all together

Now when each lesson step has been thought out and written down, it is time to put all your preparations together. Keep in mind, there are constant and variable components in the lesson plan structure. Introduction and closure are constant phases. You should not come into the class and start teaching without greeting the students, smiling and talking to them, thus preparing them for work. Write the lesson goal, objectives and outcomes on the board; explain them so students know what is expected of them today. Correspondingly, you should not abruptly interrupt your teaching and students' work when the bell rings. This would be like watching a football game which ends in the 53rd minute. So, leave a few minutes to sum up the lesson outcomes, praise the students and cheer them up. Other components may be added to the plan, depending on concrete goals and circumstances. The lesson can be completely devoted to the activities, but it would hardly be effective to focus the whole lesson only on presenting new information, without reinforcing it with activities.

Such a considered representation of the lesson plan creates a blueprint of what is to be studied that can be implemented in different ways. Once this plan is in place, it is relatively easy to infuse it with relevant content and activities. For example, the teacher can adapt the plan to a particular subject area or to special students' (e.g. ELL) needs. The actual structure of your lesson will depend on the goals, objectives, planned outcomes and actual situations in the class. This adaptation may start with teaching a carefully selected new vocabulary, proceed to tapping into students' background knowledge of the topic by questions and informal conversation, and end with playing a short video clip as an introduction to the new material.

● WHAT'S THE PLAN?

How do you think the components of the **5-Star Lesson Plan** structure might interact with each other?

_____

_____

_____

_____

_____

_____

_____

The teacher's work on the lesson should be completed with a reflection. The teacher should critically analyze the plan and its implementation in the lesson using the following questions, as recommended by NU template:

- What went well?
- What needs to be changed?
- Were learning outcomes met?
- What activities will you add, change, modify in the future?
- What can be done to follow up on the learning from this lesson?
- Who needs additional help?
- Who needs enrichment or higher level work?

What is in the Lesson Plan?

If we look closely at the **5-Star Lesson Plan**, we can observe an array of important preparation aspects (Fig 2.4):

- Lesson topic
- Academic standards
- Culturally relevant curriculum
- Goals and objectives
- Projected outcomes
- Students' characteristics

● **FIGURE 2.4   Aspects of Lesson Planning**

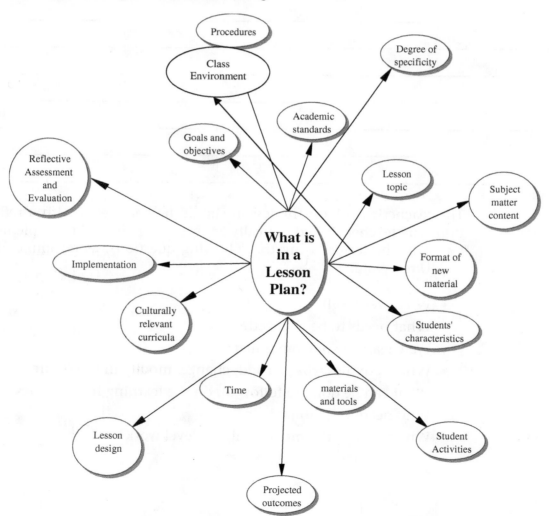

- Lesson structure
- Subject matter content
- Degree of specificity (level of complexity)
- Format of new material presentation
- Implementation methods, strategies and procedures
- Students' activities
- Supporting materials and tools, including educational technology
- Assessment and evaluation, and
- Space (physical environment that should be well organized for student activities) and time (It is always limited, and the challenge for the teacher is to use it efficiently.)

When you develop a lesson plan, remember to consider the *who, what, how* and *why* of actual classroom teaching and learning. Fundamentally you are asking, "How can I achieve successful outcomes in my class?"

Sequencing Lesson Components

What is important in the lesson plan are not only the structure of the lesson or the content and the set of activities for achieving a given goal, but also their sequence.

The main principle in sequencing the learning events in a lesson is multidirectional. The multidirectional principle can set up the events in a lesson from the presentation of new material to the assessment and evaluation of learning outcomes. A sequence can develop as follows: introduction (presentation) of the new material, then activities intended to retain the new knowledge and develop appropriate skills, and finally, appraisal of students' outcomes. You shouldn't conduct a comprehensive evaluation before the lesson material is mastered, however checking for understanding, Q&A, assessing student performance and problem-solving can be used at any stage as the students learn lesson content.

The multidirectional principle also posits that student learning is not commonly unidirectional. Depending on a given student's entry level characteristics and learning style, the teacher can present material going from the simple to the complex or from the complex to the simple, or from whole to part vs. from part to whole. (See Iterative Instructional Model in Ch. 7.) Compare these two examples.

FROM WHOLE TO PART:

In teaching literature for example, the teacher might first show a video presentation of Shakespeare's *Hamlet*. Based on this (whole) 3-hour video of a five act play, the students could then be asked to write an initial essay on only the first act or only one topic, for instance, Hamlet's relationship with his uncle.

In an ESL class, grammar patterns can be deduced from sample sentences and students will independently make their own conclusions to form the rules.

FROM PART TO WHOLE:

In introducing the Shakespearean play *Macbeth*, a famous monologue from Lady Macbeth can be initially introduced (by teacher reading the text or in a video) in order to set the predicate for studying the entire tragedy.

In teaching grammar, the rules with examples can be demonstrated and then students will be asked to build sentences of their own using these rules.

Now that you have a foundation on the overall structure of a lesson plan, it is time to look at each of the five components and understand how they are interrelated. Chapter 3 will present you in-depth information about the **5-Star Lesson Plan** *description, focusing on the subject, topic, grade level and especially on student characteristics.*

CHAPTER 3

Lesson Description

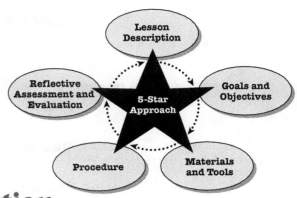

First Iteration

When you prepare your next lesson it is important to think not only about the "what" and the "how" you are going to teach, but first and foremost of the "whom" you are going to teach. Your lesson plan and your teaching will depend on the students you have in your classroom, their individual characteristics and behaviors. This chapter points to the importance of knowing when, what and to whom you are teaching. Moving from description to goals and objectives to material and tools to procedure and finally to assessment and evaluation, you can visualize and eventually implement lesson plans to best meet the needs of every student.

Date: _____

Subject: _____

Topic: _____

Grade level: _____

Class Characteristics: _____

Accommodations for ELL/Special Education Students:

_____

You will consider all these factors at the lesson plan preparation stage.

In the 2nd and 3rd iterations we will discuss various descriptors of the lesson plan in detail.

Second Iteration

• •

This part will focus on major descriptors of the lesson which affect its implementation.

Coming to Terms Over Lesson Description
• •

The lesson description includes basic information about the lesson: the date, subject, topic, grade (level of study), and class characteristics. It precedes the plan itself.

DESCRIPTION

Date: _____

Subject: _____

_____

Topic: _____

_____

Grade: _____

Class (student) characteristics: (developmental level, abilities, English learning issues)

_____

_____

_____

_____

> *Although the date describes "when," is also affects "what."*

DATE

The **date** may seem unimportant in terms of learning theory; after all, we are only considering a given day on the calendar. However, we could probably agree that class dates at the beginning of a school term tend to emphasize introductory materials, while class dates at the end of the term tend to require summative student responses. As you write the date for your class, remember that dates are used to introduce, sustain and end a sequential learning process.

> *The subject describes "what,"*
> *and interdisciplinary subject describes "how."*

SUBJECT

The **subject** being taught most likely refers to a discipline such as English, math, science, physical education, foreign languages, social science or the performing arts. Sometimes subjects, however, are best taught as interdisciplinary studies. For example, a humanities class can emanate from the combination of a history class (e.g. American History) and a literature class (e.g. American Literature). If students are offered carpentry classes, such classes can integrate math (calculations, geometry). Such an arrangement allows teaching a humanities course via thematic units across two traditionally distinct curricula. The advantage is the integration of extensive areas of knowledge. Whether one chooses to combine content areas (e.g. math and science) or include an integrated language curriculum—teaching all four language skills (listening, speaking, reading and writing) in a lesson, it may produce better learning outcomes. The choice of how a subject is to be learned is as important as what subject(s) to study.

Do you think the subject you are assigned to teach is "set in stone" or a foregone conclusion? Think again!

● WHAT'S THE PLAN?

What disciplines would you combine in order to integrate the curriculum? (**Hint:** *A math class and a physics class could be combined as an applied science course.*)

_____

_____

_____

_____

_____

TOPIC

The **topic** selected for study is yet another responsibility that has great significance in the learning process. Consider selecting the topics that become projects with both intermediate and long term goals (e.g. writing a sonnet in 12th grade English as the first installment in a class collection of poems, calculating a healthy diet, learning how to communicate about traveling, or mastering oral debates).

Of course, when choosing topics that become projects you must decide what is appropriate for learners from preschool through high school in terms of their intellectual development and social growth. It would seem that the best project topics are those that are culturally relevant, have a connection to family, community and real life, allow the learner to choose to be inspired, motivated and ultimately empowered as they meet state standards in a learning experience that provides both breadth and depth.

Topics should inform, enlighten and if intellectually stimulating, entertain. You might consider topics that grow into projects to provide the kind of developmental format needed to sustain the learning process. One might consider community based service learning projects that study, for instance, the effect of local industries on air quality or a multilingual-multicultural poetry festival.

● WHAT'S THE PLAN?

How can you make your lesson more culturally responsive? (**Hint:** *Think about finding out who your students are and what prior knowledge they bring to class.*)

_____

_____

_____

_____

_____

This approach will eventually help our students to meet their ultimate goals of becoming self-directed lifelong learners.

> *To sort students by grade is to group. No grouping should be inflexible.*
> *Mixed-age and mixed-level groupings can be of great value.*

GRADE

By **grade** we mean a level of study. The most common levels are 1st grade through 12th grade. It sounds pretty stable to pass one grade a year and enter another grade the next year. A class of a certain grade will still be heterogeneous, not homogeneous, because in it you will find students from different cultural, linguistic, socio-economic backgrounds. That diversity should be used as a benefit, rather than a hindrance, to foster students' learning.

Grade level is an organizing principle for schools. Is it always the best way to group students? Consider the notion of mixed-age, mixed level grouping and peer tutoring. When children of various ages and experiences work together, cognitive restructuring can be facilitated. When a student fails at learning a concept and falls short of the Vygotskian "zone of proximal development," the assistance of another student, who can solve problems independently, can support and model the behaviors needed to help the challenged student cross the zone.

> *If you want to learn something better, teach it.*
> (Russian proverb)

If peer tutoring is used, both the participant tutor as well as the tutee receives benefits. The tutor reinforces what he or she knows while the recipient gains new insight. In addition, peer tutoring has obvious social growth potential as students reach out to other students to assist in the learning process. So, engage students in cross-grade (cross-age) intellectual interactions whenever there is an opportunity.

In a diverse class, grouping students who are proficient in English with those who are struggling may help develop ESL language and communication skills faster. Heterogeneous groups may have more impact on achieving learning outcomes for all students than homogeneous ones.

● WHAT'S THE PLAN?

Describe an opportunity in the class you are now teaching or plan to teach where peer-tutoring could boost academic achievement as well as social growth.

_____

_____

_____

_____

CLASS CHARACTERISTICS

Class characteristics include the total number of students, their developmental level, the number of ELLs, their ESL proficiency, characteristics of exceptional and special education students, and behavioral expectations. A teacher can no longer focus on teaching a subject area or simply a standard, he or she must teach students, as noted by Eby, Herrell & Jordan in "Teaching K–12 Schools: A Reflective Approach" (2011). Knowing your students allows you to differentiate your teaching, accommodate various abilities, and use personal learning styles and behavioral characteristics to students' benefit to achieve the best outcomes.

● WHAT'S THE PLAN?

As you think about lesson plan strategies and activities, ponder the relationship between the lesson and the students' own prior knowledge. Write down an activity that you believe will "connect" with your students. (**Hint:** _In order to make your curriculum culturally responsive you need to model a real life situation that relates to the background that the students bring to the class._)

_____

_____

_____

_____

Your Turn—Practice Sheets

Please write out different description segments of a class you are teaching or plan to teach. Reflect on the options and alternatives you have for date, subject, topic, grade, and class characteristics.

DESCRIPTION

Date: _____

Subject: _____

_____

Topic: _____

_____

Grade: _____

Class characteristics: _____

_____

Third Iteration

● ●

An Overview of the 5-Star Lesson Plan

Let's begin by designing a lesson plan in your content area for your grade level using the model below by filling in the spaces. Your first try may take a few minutes, but once you become accustomed to the planning process, you will be able to design at a much quicker tempo. When planning, make an approximate projection about how long it may take you to do each activity.

1. DESCRIPTION

Date: _____

Subject: _____

_____

Topic: _____

_____

Grade: _____

Class characteristics, such as the total number of students, their developmental level, the number of ELLs, their ESL proficiency, exceptional and special education students, and behavioral expectations.

2. GOALS AND OBJECTIVES

Goals: Students will learn to:

_____

_____

_____

_____

Objectives: Students will (remember to use action words such as identify, analyze, critically assess, develop, demonstrate, etc.):

_____

_____

Outcomes: As a result of the lesson, students will be able to do the following:

_____

_____

Standards: Content standard (see your state's web site and copy appropriate standard(s)):

_____

_____

Accommodations for ELL/Special Education: Consider introducing new vocabulary, grammar points, and modeling pronunciation. Preview major new terms related to the subject and topic. This will be useful for all students, particularly for ELLs preparing for a new content area.

_____

_____

Accommodations for exceptional and special education students: Use a wide variety of methodological approaches to meet the needs per specific student characteristics and Individual Educational Plans, with particular emphasis on modes of presentation and activities.

_____

_____

3. MATERIALS AND TOOLS

Texts: _____

_____

Visuals: _____

_____

Technologies: _____

_____

Handouts, Realia and Manipulatives: _____

_____

4. PROCEDURE

Note: *Think of the block of time you have to teach a lesson and then approximate how many minutes you will need to complete each of the five steps in the procedure section.*

Introduction (. . . min.):

_____

_____

Teacher presentation (. . . min.): The teacher will:

_____

_____

Class activities (. . . min.): Students will:

_____

_____

Assessment and evaluation (. . . min.):

_____

_____

Closure (. . . min.): The teacher will sum up the lesson naming the major points discussed.

_____

_____

5. ASSESSMENT AND/OR EVALUATION

Students will be assessed or evaluated on the basis of assessments (e.g. conferences) and evaluations (e.g. testing). Recall assessments are ongoing dialogs with the learner regarding his or her strengths or weaknesses, while evaluations can be scores, rankings or grades.

Assessment: Try to find time to address each student's progress and problems

_____

_____

Testing: Identify what you are going to measure (e.g., oral presentation, written essay, project), what tools you will use (e.g., quest, test, written essay, rubric) and how (which technique you will apply, e.g., ...)

_____

_____

Let's look closely at the first phase of designing a lesson—the description.

Understanding the student population you are teaching is the first step to writing an effective lesson plan. Being aware of your students' abilities, individual characteristics, behavioral problems, prior knowledge and of what he or she needs is critical for providing adequate accommodations. This information will allow you to devise a lesson plan to teach the most enriched curriculum via the widest variety of methodological approaches to every student in the class. In the next chapter you will learn how to write effective goals and objectives that actually define what you are going to accomplish in your lesson.

CHAPTER 4

....

Goals, Objectives and Outcomes

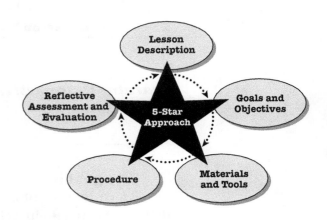

First Iteration

●●

Every lesson has a purpose and an aim. This means each time you teach you should have goals and objectives. You need to understand, however, not only where you are going in the lesson, but also what your students will accomplish in the end, which is identified in the learning outcomes. Just like a captain of a ship, knowing where you are going (goal), what you must accomplish to get there (objectives), and what you will get from your voyage/how you will benefit from your voyage (outcomes), a teacher must have a firm idea of how to launch a successful lesson plan.

Each time you teach you should have goals, objectives and outcomes at the top of your lesson plan. So, what is a *goal,* how is it different than an *objective,* and what do we achieve in the *outcome*?

Say you are going to travel to San Francisco from San Diego to ride the cable cars. Obviously the goal is to enjoy the cable car ride in San Francisco. With any goal the focus is on the ends rather than the means.

On the other hand, the objective is to get there, so you should set a measurable (502 miles), and time-efficient (8.5 hours) travel plan based on the transportation mode you will use, for instance a car. The objective is clear and specific. The focus is on the means rather than the end.

And what will the *outcome* of your travel be? Evidently, satisfaction at achieving your goal, new experiences, knowledge, and skills you will be able to use in your life and which you will share with your family and friends.

Goals: Students will learn to _____

Objectives: Students will . . . (analyze, develop, prove, investigate,

evaluate, . . .) _____

Learning Outcomes: As a result of the lesson, students will be able to . . . (explain, describe, create, produce, compare, demonstrate, . . .)

So, a **goal** is the strategic, ultimate purpose of the lesson.

An **objective** of a lesson is one of the specific, explicit, intermediate aims that help achieve particular, pre-designed outcomes of a lesson determined by the broader goal of the lesson. The objective also identifies the mean of achieving the planned outcome.

A **learning outcome** is one of the lesson's results. It is, in fact, the objective implemented through effective instruction and student learning.

In the 2nd and 3rd iterations of this chapter we will examine in more depth the concepts of goals and objectives and how they relate to prior knowledge and current standards. We will delve into the notion of tangible objectives and the concept of basic vocabulary for any given lesson you may teach.

Second Iteration

• •

This part will examine the concepts of goals, objectives, outcomes, prior knowledge, and standards.

Goals: Students will learn to _____

_____

Objectives: Students will . . . (identify general behavioral objectives, such as analyze, demonstrate, prove, create, etc.):

_____

_____

Learning Outcomes: As a result of the lesson, students will be able to . . . (explain, describe, create, produce, compare, evaluate, . . .)

_____

_____

Standards: _____

_____

Coming to Terms Over Goals, Objectives and Learning Outcomes

• •

Setting goals and objectives, and defining the learning outcomes for your lesson are, probably, the most critical tasks in lesson planning. They are the **guidelines** for you and for your students in making their learning more meaningful and effective. Goals, objectives and outcomes must be very clear to students who need to understand the lesson's expectations. At the same time, the outcomes should be quantifiable and measurable, which will give you grounds for objective evaluation. Before you identify the goals, objectives and outcomes of the lesson, you have to revisit students' prior knowledge which will help you do a better job.

Prior Knowledge

Prior knowledge is the understanding that students bring to classroom. New knowledge begins to be understood when the learner uses his or her prior knowledge to make out familiar patterns of thought within the new knowledge in order to interpret new or enhanced meanings. This is called bridging the new learning to the past knowledge. Within the constructivist framework, prior knowledge is a significant factor in the learning process.

When you, as the teacher, set the goals and objectives, and define the outcomes, they should determine what you expect students to learn and be able to do by the end of this lesson. At the same time, they must rely on prior knowledge which is a scaffold for the new one. It is not a very simple task but it will give students more confidence in attacking the new knowledge. However, if you do it right, it will help you achieve your aim.

Goals

A **goal** is the strategic, ultimate purpose of the lesson. Goals establish the aim, reason and rationale for what you and your students will engage in during the lesson. When setting goals, ask yourself, *where you will take your students*, and *what will you expect them to gain*. The goals are typically defined as broad targets related to state or national curriculum standards. For instance: "Students will understand the function of all three branches of government in the United States of America." A lesson usually has one goal.

● WHAT'S THE PLAN?

Write some goals for a class you are teaching or intend to teach in the future (**Hint:** *Think big as in an encompassing state standard.*)

_____

_____

_____

_____

Objectives

An **objective** of a lesson is one of the specific, explicit, intermediate aims that help achieve particular, pre-designed outcomes of a lesson. The objectives for a lesson plan are determined by the broader goal of the lesson.

The objectives focus on particular knowledge and skills pertaining to this goal and involve higher order thinking. To identify the objectives, you should break the goal into a few meaningful interrelated aims or purposes.

A well-defined objective should lead to a measurable outcome in order for the learner as well as the evaluator to determine learning has taken place. Therefore, an objective becomes the means for measuring success upon reaching an outcome. The action plan is about how to achieve the goals using the objectives as intermediate aims or steps. E.g., Students will analyze a...; explain the function, design a plan, create a model, apply the new knowledge in a particular situation, etc. A lesson usually has several objectives.

● **FIGURE 4.1**

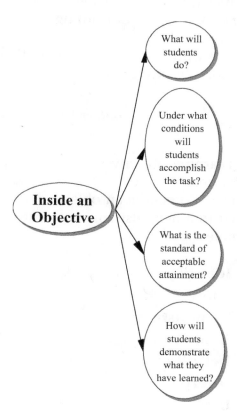

● WHAT'S THE PLAN?

Write some objectives for the goal or goals for a class you are teaching or intend to teach in the future (***Hint:*** *Check the goal or goals you have already written in Chapter 3.*)

_____

_____

_____

_____

Having objectives in mind helps you to focus on the right strategies, activities and tools.

People often confuse actions with objectives. It is a common mistake to set objectives denoting them as verbs indicating what students will do during the lesson, (e.g., "Students will read, write, present, etc."). These are, in fact, the procedures described in the lesson, the activities that help to achieve the goals and objectives, however they are *not* the purpose of learning, rather the means of attaining the outcomes.

It is worthwhile to remember that lesson outcomes are identified by lesson objectives.

> *An objective is a planned outcome.*

Learning objectives in general and behavioral objectives in particular need to be clear, concise, observable, measurable, and student-centered. To denote an objective, you should use an action verb connected to a demonstrable outcome, which is usually measurable. For example:

- **Identify**
- **Show**
- **Demonstrate**
- **Describe**
- **Define**
- **Interpret**
- **Use**
- **Apply**

- **Analyze**
- **Synthesize**
- **Explain**
- **Prove**
- **Create**
- **Design**

The goals and objectives should be practical, realistic, and originate from real-life needs and situations, if possible. For example:

- In an ESL class, we will learn how to order food in an American restaurant.
- Students will be able to apply a mathematical formula in solving a problem, e.g., calculating how to save up money when purchasing an iPhone.

To clearly set the objectives, use Mager's Performance Objectives (Mager 1962) and Bloom's Taxonomy (Bloom 1956). Mager outlines three parts of an objective: identify the learner, identify the situation in which the learning takes place, and state the criterion for acceptable performance. The Taxonomy is helpful for categorizing levels of abstraction of the questions that commonly occur in educational settings.

Learning Outcomes

A **learning outcome** is one of the lesson's results. It is identified in the objective as a specific aim which is a part of the overall lesson's goal. Therefore, an outcome is, in reality, the implemented objective achieved through effective instruction and student learning. A lesson usually has several planned outcomes corresponding to the objectives.

A learning outcome is defined as a student's newly developed ability to demonstrate and apply the new knowledge and skills, for instance, "The student will be able to design a device, build it using available parts, explain its construction and work, and demonstrate its function." An outcome should be quantifiable so it could be measured for evaluation. The outcome can be measured in quantity, volume, and time, which can be calculated and expressed in points or grades, while to evaluate the quality the teacher might use the rubric which assigns specific points or grades to each particular characteristic. (Examples of evaluation criteria are described in Ch. 7. Assessment and Evaluation.)

As a teacher you strive to enable students to learn to do something concrete and involve higher order thinking. Therefore you should be very clear in your statement of the outcomes in what you expect your students to do as a result of achieving the objectives in this particular lesson.

There is usually one goal for a particular lesson, (e.g. "Students will learn how to form the plural of nouns," or "Students will learn to identify and describe the location of objects in space," or "Students will learn to divide integers." However, there is usually more than one objective that helps to make the goal attainable, and, correspondingly, several outcomes. Each objective targets one of the components of the overall goal. For example, for the first of the abovementioned goals, the objectives might be set as follows:
Students will

- Identify the difference between singular and plural nouns,
- Describe *singularia* and *pluralia tantum*,
- Explain the grammar rule of forming a plural noun.

The outcomes of reaching these objectives will be as follows:
Students will

- Be able to form a plural noun from a singular one,
- Demonstrate their new knowledge and skills through using nouns in plural both in oral and written speech.

When setting the outcomes, ask yourself, what will students be able to do as a result of this lesson, under what conditions will they accomplish the task, what is the standard of acceptable attainment, how will your students demonstrate what they have learned in the lesson, and finally, how will you measure their new knowledge and skills as compared to the preset outcomes? To answer these questions, the outcomes must be specific, tangible, and preferably quantifiable.

Remember, the lesson's goal, objectives and outcomes should all be aligned.

> *Lesson outcomes should match lesson objectives.*

Standards

An academic **standard** identifies subject area content which should be aligned with evaluation tools. Academic standards define both breadth and depth of knowledge. State standards typically delineate

● **FIGURE 4.2   Academic Standards**

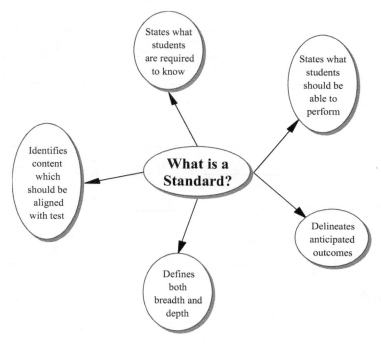

anticipated outcomes. In simple terms they state what students are required to know and what students should be able to perform.

Therefore, standards are not about methodological approaches (the *how* something is done), but are generally discipline-specific and therefore curricular and process oriented (the *what*) in nature (Fig 4.2).

> ***Standards inform lessons plans and act to gauge academic performance.***

It is good to remember, when setting the goal, objectives and outcomes, that you should align them with the standards but not use them as the lesson's objectives as the latter might be different from the former in interpretation or form.

Your Turn—Practice Sheets

Now build the second step of the lesson plan by adding your goals, objectives, outcomes and standards to lessons you plan to teach in the future. Please take care that they are all consistent and aligned.

I. GOALS, OBJECTIVES AND OUTCOMES

Goals: _____

_____

_____

Objectives: _____

_____

_____

Outcomes: _____

_____

_____

Standards: _____

_____

_____

Third Iteration

• •

This part will explain how to assess students' prior knowledge, discuss tangible objectives, and help understand how to develop basic vocabulary.

When we discuss prior knowledge, let us look at a tool you can use in the classroom to access prior knowledge. The K-W-L chart created by Ogle (1986) is one way to approach prior knowledge. Learners relate their prior knowledge and engage in the learning process when they state what they **Know**; then set goals specifying what they **Want** to learn; and after intervening instruction declare what they have **Learned**.

Learners make reflective assessments using higher order critical thinking skills to construct meaning from new information. The worksheet below (Fig. 4.3) is a tool that can be given to every learner to ferret out prior knowledge, aspirations and a reflective assessment of what comprehension has been developed.

● **FIGURE 4.3   K-W-L Chart**

K What I *Know*	W What I *Want* to Know	L What I *Learned*

Tangible Objectives

Objectives Should Be TANGIBLE. Think of the acronym **TANGIBLE** when devising your lesson plan.

A **TANGIBLE** objective should: target, acculturate, negotiate, guide, integrate, build, limit and engage (Fig. 4.4).

TARGETS

For example, when a teacher simply states she wants her students to demonstrate their knowledge of United States history, there is an obvious lack of specificity as to why they should do it and how it could be accomplished. Students have a much better idea about how to demonstrate their knowledge if the teacher provides options.

Possible Objective: You are president of the United States of America in 1861. The country is on the verge of a civil war. Come up with five realistic proposals for the Congress on how to avoid the bloodshed.

Such an objective which invites students to role playing not only gives meaning to students' activities, but also increases their motivation to accomplish the desired outcome.

● **FIGURE 4.4   Tangible Ojbective**

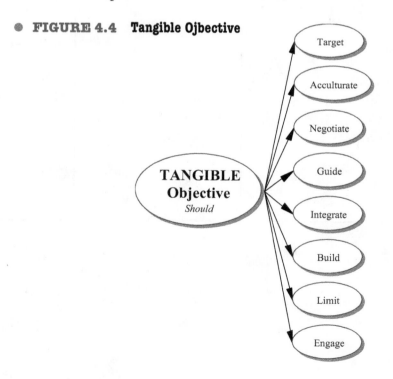

ACCULTURATES

Making connections among contrasting cultural identities that have very different cultural beliefs, communication modes, and interpersonal rapport is essential in a student population ever more culturally and linguistically diverse. Objectives should encourage more team approaches in the classroom so that students could maintain their identity while they learn to appreciate the cultural norms of other classmates through interaction and communication with them.

Objectives need to recognize and endorse multiple identities in students without valuing one identity over another. Objectives can draw on authentic personal experiences while fostering warm relationships with family and community and encouraging students to appreciate and maintain their own cultural heritage as they learn another.

> *Possible Objective:* Interview a family member who was alive during the Vietnam War. Ask that person how the war affected his or her life. Offer a discussion of the topic in the class.
>
> Or,
>
> Interview a family member or an acquaintance who was not born in the United States and had lived most of her/his life outside this country about how people in that country regarded the United States at that time. Share your findings with the class.

NEGOTIATES

Students should be involved in setting some parts of an objective. People become responsible when they have an opportunity to be accountable. For students to be engaged they must relate in a personal way to what is being taught.

> *Possible Objective:* Do you believe in being healthy? Please share with us your views on this issue: choose whether to write a 1,000 word paper or deliver a 15-minute Power Point presentation on a personal exercise and nutrition plan.

GUIDES

An objective should guide a student through a developmental task via the use of critical thinking skills. Learning progresses to the extent that it takes place via analysis, synthesis, and reflection. Thinking rather than repeating, regurgitating or parroting is necessary if the objective is to guide the student academically.

Possible Objective: Give your arguments pro or con on capital punishment by participating in a Socratic dialogue. Articulate at least two thoughtful questions or statements about capital punishment within this conversation to demonstrate rigorous thinking as the student moves from the unexamined to the examined.

INTEGRATES

An objective should bring together various features of what is to be studied pointing to meaningful associations with authentic local and global concerns. Objectives should be geared to the real world where the interdependence of knowledge is a reflection of how the brain interconnects reality.

Possible Objective: Students will begin a school rose garden in order to improve the scenic environment of the community. Students will write a poem about the beauty of the rose garden after the ground area is plotted; the number of plants decided, planting and watering is calculated and assigned. **Note:** *This objective integrates, math, language arts, ecology and service to the community.*

BUILDS

An objective should build on the experiences students bring to class. It should also permit students to create or construct their own new understandings or knowledge via a synthesis and special higher order interaction between the student's previous knowledge and new ideas and/or activities.

Possible Objective: Student teams will build containers to protect an egg to be dropped from a height of 50 feet. Innovative problem-solving approaches and collaboration with other team members is required.

LIMITS

Time and length of an activity are inherently limited because objectives are finite. When you plan a lesson, it is useful to allocate an approximate time to all lesson activities to see if you meet the goals and objectives. Measurements taken of scores or rankings at the completion of a certain objective make up a part of a student's total evaluation.

> *Possible Objective:* Students have one hour to complete 10 questions on a short answer quiz, which is worth 10% of their semester grade.

ENGAGES

Student engagement to fulfill an objective is based on motivation. Genuine motivation occurs via student choice. Activities chosen must set an environment where students elect to become inspired, motivated, interested and ultimately empowered. Recall that unlike a mere incentive, genuine motivation emanates inside a person providing internal rewards. The staying power of motivation is comparably stronger and more long-lasting than that of an incentive (Fig. 4.5).

> *Possible Objective:* Students reach out to their community to create a 30-minute concert of holiday songs to sing at children's hospitals in the area.

● **FIGURE 4.5**   **Incentive and Motivation (from Ryan, 2005)**

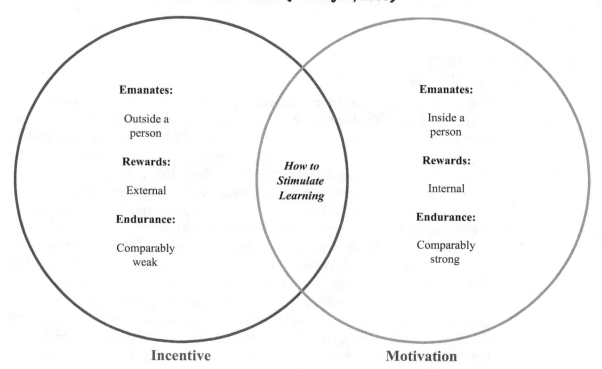

● WHAT'S THE PLAN?

How does a student become motivated? (**Hint:** *The common notion of a teacher motivating a student is erroneous. Actually what a teacher does is set an environment where a student elects to become motivated. So what kind of a classroom environment will lead the student to self-motivate?*)

_____

_____

_____

_____

Remember, intrinsic motivation based on the learner's realistic needs and personal interests will always be more effective than an external one, coming from the teacher, such as task, assignment, grade or praise. Intrinsic motivation emerges when the student associates himself or herself with the personally meaningful task, e.g., "If you decided to be a teacher, what, in your opinion, are the most important teacher qualities that you need to develop?," or, "You are a teacher in high school. How are you going to engage your students in community work?"

Basic Vocabulary

The idea behind **basic vocabulary** is to make information meaningful to every student by defining ideas and activities via a fundamental terminology. Every student, and ELL in particular, enters school with diverse, culturally based experiences with school and language. Therefore, you can teach vocabulary using English language, appealing to the learners' first language whenever necessary, and also utilizing visuals, demonstrations, body language and manipulatives to make the new words comprehensible to all students.

Teaching a basic vocabulary should take into considerations the students' previous experiences in order to analogize within the process of learning new terms. In terms of the ELL, ideally these students continue to acquire English while they enhance literacy in their native language and knowledge of their native culture (Fig 4.6). The result of a well structured bilingual program can be a bi-literate, bicultural student who can best serve his community and his country.

● **FIGURE 4.6**   **Teaching the Vocabulary**

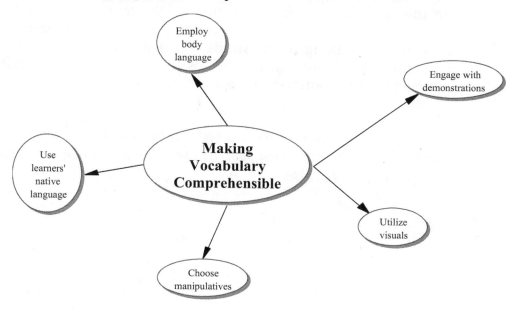

Research states, reading in one's first language spurs the acquisition of the reading ability in one's second language. Therefore, use the first language to accelerate acquisition of the second language.

This approach, however, is useful in the initial stages of language development. As soon as students develop basic proficiency, it is necessary to exclude the first language from the use in the classroom. It will enhance their achievements in the second language.

How do you select the vocabulary for the lesson? You know your students' strengths and weaknesses, and are certainly aware of what they can do and what they can't. This will be useful for all students, particularly for English Language Learners preparing for a new content area.

When preparing a lesson plan, review the topic and the teaching materials, primarily the texts, and select the words students may have never encountered. They may be general use words, or may pertain to a specific area of knowledge, e.g. math, science, history terms. Select those they will need to understand the lesson, and make up a list. This list should be supplemented with pictures, graphs, and other illustrations that may help students to perceive the meaning of each word. Sometimes you may want to use translation into the students' first language, if you feel it will clarify the meaning. Write these words on the board before the lesson, prepare illustrations, manipulatives, PowerPoint slides or use the computer with an LSD projector to explain the meaning of the words and demonstrate their use. Urge your students to write all new words in their personal vocabularies (notebooks) and continuously repeat them.

Now as you know what the goals, objectives and learning outcomes are and how to set them in your lesson plan, let's see what lesson materials and tools you will need to achieve them.

CHAPTER 5

Learning Materials and Tools

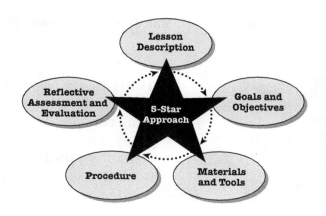

First Iteration

From the newest 21st century technology to traditional textbooks, the materials and tools which today's teacher can access provide a wide array of resources to enhance the learning process. In our digital age we can see and hear video via the Internet, instantaneously communicate via a cell phone or by email with a friend who is 10,000 miles away, and access an online class virtually whenever we want and as many times as we want to reinforce learning. We can do it now even without sitting in the classroom or at a home computer via mobile technology. As our tools become more interactive, the role of the teacher does not diminish. As a selector of what web sites to visit, the facilitator and resident expert in class forums, and as an assessor of learning, you can explore and access virtually limitless resources in cyberspace.

Teaching and learning requires numerous and varied materials and tools.

Materials include anything carrying information or used for constructing knowledge and developing skills, such as texts or any other reading materials, visuals, handouts, realia (real life objects used in classroom activities), art and crafts supplies (materials for drawing, coloring, constructing, such as paper, wood, clay, fabric, cardboard, etc), manipulatives (objects used to build a structure, for example Lego blocks, flash cards, beans), as well as DVD discs, memory/flash cards, streaming video, phonograms, video recordings, text messages, web-based resources, computer apps courses and other information using electronic format.

Tools are teacher and student instruments that can be simple, such as whiteboards, pens, rulers, textbooks, reference books, or more complex tools (which are referred to as educational technology) when based on electronics, mechanics, optics, such as computers, iPads and iPods, mobile phones, calculators, DVD players, overhead projectors, TVs, computer programs, and Internet. Materials and tools may enhance learning.

Materials: _____

Tools: _____

Until recently we thought only about printed text when talking about literacy. Today we also have computer literacy (the ability to operate a computer) and visual literacy (the ability to extract or create meaning from images using electronic devices).

The term **technology** simply means a tool, though a sophisticated one. The computer and the Internet are learning tools as we look through a monitor and visit informational sites in our journey through cyberspace.

In the 2nd and 3rd Iterations of this chapter we will discuss technical and educational potentials of the materials and tools, and their applications in teaching and learning.

Second Iteration

• •

In this iteration you will review a variety of materials and tools you will use in teaching your lessons which will help students achieve their learning outcomes.

Both teachers and students need various materials and tools for their teaching and learning.

Materials and Tools
• •

Lesson Topic: _____

_____

Lesson Goal, Objectives and Outcomes: _____

_____

_____

Texts: _____

_____

_____

Visuals: _____

_____

_____

Technologies: _____

_____

_____

Handouts, Realia and Manipulatives: _____

_____

_____

Coming to Terms Over Materials and Tools

Teaching and learning requires numerous materials and tools. **Materials** include anything carrying information or used for constructing knowledge and developing skills:

- Texts or any other reading materials
- Visuals
  - Drawings
  - Pictures
  - Graphs
  - Posters
  - Albums
- Audio materials
  - Audio records of conversations, speeches, plays and lessons on DVD or from the internet
- Handouts (ready-made or self-developed resources to provide content and support for the activities)
- Realia (real-life objects used in classroom activities)
- Art and crafts supplies (materials for drawing, coloring, constructing, such as paper, wood, clay, fabric, cardboard, etc.).
- Manipulatives (objects used to build a structure, for example blocks, flash cards, beans, Legos)
- Costumes and masks

Tools are teacher and student instruments that can be simple, such as whiteboards, pens, rulers, textbooks, reference books, or more complex tools (which are referred to as educational technology) when based on electronics, mechanics, optics, such as computers, calculators, DVD or CD players, iPods, iPads, iPhones, overhead projectors, TVs, computer programs, and Internet. Materials and tools help enhance learning.

If until recently we thought only about printed text when talking about literacy, in our days we also have *computer literacy* (the ability to operate a computer) and *visual literacy* (the ability to extract or create meaning from images using electronic devices). Today's students are more accustomed to communicating via mobile devices, hearing digitalized sound in their earphones, scanning digital text on the computer screen, and analyzing images on their computer monitor (or ipod, ipad, iphone and other gadgets) rather than reading text printed on the paper. Therefore, we have to integrate digital texts, sounds and images and communication into teaching and learning.

The term **technology** simply means a tool, though a sophisticated one. Just as a knife and fork represent Western technology as eating tools, the computer and the Internet represent learning tools as we look at a video monitor and visit internet sites in our journey through cyberspace.

No doubt, the role of electronic technology is growing in society and in the classroom. Ever newly emergent and more refined devices that relay both sound and image make it important for teachers to consider how technology can enhance the learning process. As we are moving from text-based information to multimedia digital information, we need to use effective ways of information search, selection, evaluation, processing, presenting, retaining and applying.

Educational Technology Applications In the Lesson

Educational Technology (ET) includes technical, programming and instructional tools used together with human resources in teaching and learning. Technology applications are implemented in the lesson through a research-based set of strategies and techniques to efficiently solve classroom problems emerging in instructional, research and organizational situations.

Today we use five major groups of ET in instructional practice:

1. Audio technology—ipods, DVD and CD players, that are used to record and play audio text (dialogues, monologues), drama, music and sound;

2. Video technology—DVD, VCR, ipads, camcorders and TV that help to record and play dynamic pictures on video;

3. Projection technology—slide and overhead projectors, as well as LCD projectors for demonstrating text and images on a large screen;

4. Information and computer technology (ICT)—computers that offer computer-based lessons, computer games, virtual reality, multimedia, automated/computerized tests, word processors, spreadsheets, databases, graphics and presentation software;

5. Telecommunications technology—the Internet and WWW that provide online courses, various distributed web-based educational resources, web browsers for searching the web, email for electronic communication, videoconferencing for group video meetings, streaming video, bulletin boards, whiteboards (dabble boards), communication tools for interaction, such as chat, texting, social networks, wikis, tweets, etc.

These technologies can be used in all phases of the lesson. They are particularly effective in the presentation phase, in the activities phase, in students' independent work, and in evaluation.

● WHAT'S THE PLAN?

As you develop a lesson plan, think what ETs you might use to make teaching new content more effective? (**Hint:** *Think what kind of information students will perceive, understand and retain better due to a particular ET.*)

_____

_____

_____

_____

_____

Teachers who use ET expand the opportunities for productive teaching and learning, and make teaching and learning more efficient. You can diversify your methodological approaches via effective technology-based content presentation, varied and result-oriented practical activities implemented on the computer, access to virtually unlimited web-based information resources, automated and efficient assessment and evaluation, plus wide and instantaneous communication capabilities.

Technology should be integrated in teaching and learning whenever the teacher sees an opportunity to enhance the learning environment. Use of ET provides the tools you may need to overcome the context-reduced limitations of the classroom instruction, create a simulated thematic virtual environment or a real-life situation, and to set an atmosphere where students have more opportunities to engage in the learning process.

Many of the teaching and learning activities in class, as well as in homework, can be more effectively performed with ET that without it. You can use ET in the following:

- Information activities, such as information search and processing, for which students can use the computer and the World Wide Web;

- Information presentation—computer, ipad, DVD, CD-ROM, CD player, TV and projectors;

- Textual activities, such as texting, text processing, editing and generating, utilizing text editor or spell check in the computer;
- Learning activities proper: question-answer, drill, practice, problem-solving, role-playing and simulation operating a computer, tape recorder, video camera, VCR and DVD players;
- Communication activities, such as dialogue, group discussion and conference via email, chat, threaded discussion, blog, wikis, video conference and telephone conversation;
- Assessment and evaluation activities—continuous assessment and automated computerized tests.

● WHAT'S THE PLAN?

When preparing a lesson plan, think what kinds of learning activities can be performed in the class when you use ETs? *(Hint: Consider student activities you often offer such as: information search and processing, preparing assignments, communicating and skill development.)*

_____

_____

_____

_____

_____

Handouts, Realia and Manipulatives

The term **handouts** usually refers to the materials given to students that can extend or enhance the curriculum. A handout can simply contain information (a printed text, a map of California, references to support the activities or the lyrics to *O Susanna*). Likewise, a handout may, as in the workbook section of this text, give the student an opportunity to "fill in the blanks."

Whether handouts are simply information, or require work to be done, or are a combination of both, there is one prerequisite to adhere to: Handouts must not lead to mere information but to meaning thus engaging students in interaction with the content.

Realia are various real-life objects that help make learning more realistic. They are critical for bridging real life into the learning and can include various things: price lists from the stores that can be used in mathematics class, menus from restaurants in an ESL lesson on how to order a meal, a collection of stones in a science lesson in geology, or chemical substances for chemistry experiments. Children's toys make excellent realia substitutes, for instance, you can use toy telephones for setting up a dialogue in the class, or a doll to illustrate body parts, or toy furniture to talk about the house.

Manipulatives are items that students can play with to aid the learning process. For example, they are objects commonly used to build structures as with blocks, e.g., Lego building set, or to test recollection as with flash cards, or to count up tangible sums as with beans.

● WHAT'S THE PLAN?

As you develop a lesson plan, think about the tools you have at your disposal in the classroom that can better develop student knowledge and skills and let you focus more on creative activities (**Hint:** *Think about using instructional tools, including ET, when it can do a better job and save time.*)

_____

_____

_____

_____

Your Turn—Practice Sheets

Select materials and tools for the lesson on a certain topic. Align them with the goal, objectives and learning outcomes.

Topic: _____

_____

Goal, Objectives and Learning Outcomes: _____

_____

_____

_____

Texts: _____

_____

_____

Visuals and Realia: _____

_____

_____

_____

Technologies: _____

_____

_____

_____

Handouts and Manipulatives: _____

_____

_____

_____

Third Iteration

● ●

This iteration will help you understand various technology applications in teaching and learning.

The Role of Technology

Though technology is making teaching and learning more effective, we have to realize technology alone cannot improve what people know or how they learn. It has been said that, "A fool with tools is still a fool." Technology can serve the learner well when it is:

- Self-directed (searching the Internet for ideas to bring to science or English class)
- Contextual (watching a video of *Romeo and Juliet* for literature class, or a video *Nicholas and Alexandra* about Russian czars in a history class)
- Group-oriented (producing and directing a school concert via DVD or engaging in a test-based discussion on the internet)
- Reflective (using a computer to create a plan or a project and then reflect on it)
- Informed (checking your teacher's online class site for assignments and grades)

In all of these activities technology can encourage the growth of students':

- Higher-order thinking skills (analyzing, synthesizing and evaluating)
- Problem-solving skills (devising solution sets)
- Critical thinking skills (selecting the information from the web for your class work and assessing your peers' posts in the discussion)
- Knowledge construction (building knowledge via interacting with web-based resources and with other people)

- Collaborative learning (communicating and working with others to increase productivity and achieve a common goal)
- Instant access and communication (emailing or chatting with peers, interacting with people over social networks, or accessing and working with images, text and sound)

ET APPLICATIONS

Let us consider a few examples of ET application.

WORD PROCESSOR

The word processor's main use is text generation and processing (Fig. 5.1).

You can utilize it as an educational tool for writing instruction, composition skills formation, vocabulary and grammar practice, and project development. Along with developing writing skills, working with the text indirectly helps to develop reading skills as well due to skill transfer. Working with the text on a word processor helps one stimulate thinking (Fig 5.2).

● **FIGURE 5.1 Word Processor Applications: Textual Activities**

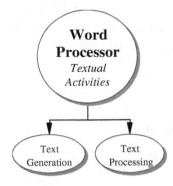

● **FIGURE 5.2 Word Processor Applications: Other Activities**

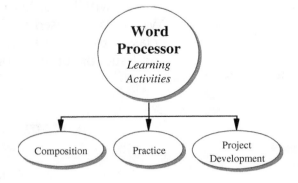

● WHAT'S THE PLAN?

As you develop a lesson plan, think how you can use a computer for students' work with the text. (**Hint:** *Think about usual activities, such as creating an outline, writing an essay, preparing a report, developing a project, or composing a letter.*)

_____

_____

_____

_____

_____

_____

VIDEO

Video can be used for new material presentation (both in visual and audio-visual formats), for creating the context of student activities (e.g., communicative activities), for portraying and simulating real-life situations (Fig 5.3), and for self-assessment.

Activities:

- Show a documentary or a movie on the topic related to the lesson which will help connect instruction to real-life situations. Video can be used for content presentation and as material for class activities or homework, (e.g., for writing an essay, discussing an issue, or solving a problem).

● **FIGURE 5.3   Video Applications**

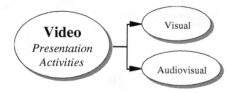

- Use video clips to demonstrate models of real-life activities, (e.g., shopping, cooking, eating at the restaurant, visiting a doctor, making cars, building houses, etc.). Then use activities, such as case study or role playing to develop the necessary knowledge and skills. These models can help students be more creative in their assignments and projects which can be made more meaningful and true-to-life.

- Demonstrate various communicative situations where native speakers of the language communicate on certain topics. That will give students samples for imitating speech patterns and later for more consistent participation in dialogues and group discussions.

- Integrate silent video for productive activities, such as describing a realistic situation or writing an audio script in which students write conversations for the actors.

- Students may learn how to perform some tasks in various realistic situations by recording their performance on the video and then analyzing it and reflecting on it. E.g., video recording their teaching a lesson and then doing self-assessment.

Video can be integrated in individual and group learning activities such as problem-solving, role-playing, simulation games and group discussions (Fig.5.4).

The latter application is particularly important for situated learning when a videotaped real-life situation is used for group analysis and discussion. For example, a video about the rain forest may be used for research and project development, while a video about a French restaurant serves as an excellent model for students learning how to speak French in the dining situations. Student activity (e.g., building a machine, or teaching younger kids) recorded on the video may serve as a material for a case study and discussion.

● **FIGURE 5.4   Video Applications: Creative Activities**

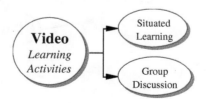

● WHAT'S THE PLAN?

As you develop a lesson plan, think how you can use video demonstrations to improve your content presentation and enhance student work. (**Hint:** *Think about enhancing your lecture or text presentation with video clips, or offering students a video for a discussion or problem solving.*)

_____

_____

_____

_____

EMAIL

Email is used predominantly as a communication tool for individual and group message exchange. At the same time, it is a great instrument for reading and writing instruction, tutoring, consultations, Q&A exercises, problem-solving and role playing (Fig 5.5).

Activities:

* Advise students to exchange information for assignments and home work.
* Suggest that students collaboratively develop a project sharing their individual contributions with the team.

● FIGURE 5.5   Email Applications

- Establish active email communication in the class so that students create a learning community outside school where they can discuss assignments, share their work, problems and their solutions.
- In an ESL class, get in touch with a class studying English as a Foreign Language in another country, and create a continuous communication in English among students. Develop a joint pen-pal project. It may help develop understanding of other countries and their culture.

● WHAT'S THE PLAN?

As you develop a lesson plan, think how you can use email for creating a learning community and for more effective student work. (**Hint:** *Think about making your students work in teams in a cooperative model when doing out-of-class assignments.*)

_____

_____

_____

_____

SKYPE

Skype allows establish visual communication between two people. Use Skype for advising and consultations. Students can use Skype for interaction and collaboration in pairs

SOCIAL MEDIA

Web-based social networking through online services like Facebook, Twitter, Wikis, LinkedIn, MySpace, Google+, etc. provide means for users to interact over the internet using e-mail and instant messaging. Young people use networking as a new entertainment for fun, for socializing and satisfying their need for interacting and talking to others. Social networking offers opportunities to share interests and activities, thus attracting people through their curiosity. A major feature of networking is it is self-initiated, therefore it is intrinsically motivated and has value for the learner. It also relieves an isolation factor. Students may have an individual communication and learning space which provides ownership for everyone.

Social networking in school can be used for organizing students' collaboration on the assignments and for discussing class matters. There may be a meeting place for parents to communicate among themselves and with the teacher.

● WHAT'S THE PLAN?

As you develop a lesson plan, think how you can use social networking for engaging students in group work. (**Hint:** *Think about integrating social networking in student assignments and activities.*)

_____

_____

_____

_____

WEB SEARCH ENGINES

More and more information can be found on the Internet. It has become easier to search for information on the Internet using Web search engines (Google, Yahoo, Bing, Ask, Mozilla Firefox, etc.) than to use the traditional library. Any learning activity that needs information can benefit from web-based resources. Students enjoy surfing the web, so the activities that rely on the use of internet resources may create positive attitude towards the assignment. These activities, however, are better used in students out-of-class work to save on class time. Students can integrate live links in the texts they write, creating hypertext products.

● WHAT'S THE PLAN?

As you develop a lesson plan, think how you can use web browsing for effective student work. (**Hint:** *Think about integrating web-based resources in student assignments and activities.*)

_____

_____

_____

_____

● **FIGURE 5.6　Audio Applications**

AUDIO

Audio technology, such as DVD players, ipods and radio can be used for playing audio text, listening to broadcasts, sounds and music, and recording student speech. It is used in second language study for developing listening skills, pronunciation, audio memory, creating sound pictures, making learning more realistic and effective (Fig. 5.6).

Activities:

- Students' listening to recordings and repeating sounds, words and sentences helps develop listening and pronunciation skills.

- Students listening to a song, then learning to sing it (in chorus and individually) helps develop pronunciation, vocabulary, grammar and also cultural appreciation.

- Students' listening to radio develops their understanding of oral speech and improves their listening and communication skills. Besides, it enhances their knowledge (e.g., news, topical talks).

- Students recording their speech and then playing it back teaches them listening, pronunciation, articulation and self-evaluation skills.

- Playing various music in the class during some activities, (e.g., during writing and silent games, especially classical music by Mozart, Haydn and Handel) was shown to enhance student learning through positively affecting their emotions.

- Playing recordings of various sounds, (e.g., bird singing, wind blowing, sounds of the water, traffic in the city, kitchen work, etc.), allows to recreate real-life sounds and thus introduces reality into the classroom by making learning connected to actual experiences, especially when used in appropriate situations.

● WHAT'S THE PLAN?

As you develop a lesson plan, think how you can use sounds, audio text and music for developing student knowledge and skills. (**Hint:** *Think about integrating the sounds of your students' popular electronic gadgets in their learning.*)

_____

_____

_____

_____

PROJECTION TECHNOLOGY

Projection technology includes devices that help demonstrate enlarged pictures on a big screen. Big size images produce a stronger impression on the viewers than small pictures in books. Projection devices are made up of overhead projectors that use transparences, slide projectors that use slides made with a camera, and LCD projectors that project images from the computer. Movies in the theater are shown with projection devices too.

Large pictures are useful to show images of small or detailed objects, tables, charts and figures. It may be effective when explaining new material that needs a higher resolution. Such enlarged pictures can also be used in discussions, role playing, problem-solving for demonstrating an image of an object or situation (Fig. 5.7). It is very popular and effective to use PowerPoint slides in new material presentation, as well as in student activities, such a project demonstration.

● **FIGURE 5.7   Projection Applications**

● WHAT'S THE PLAN?

As you develop a lesson plan, think how you can use projection technology to better explain the content and engage students. (**Hint:** *Think about using simple ways of demonstrating large images.*)

_____

_____

_____

_____

_____

ET applications should not be limited only to the delivery or presentation of information, or to the development of certain skills. In fact, they can greatly affect the emotional state and cognitive processes of the learner. Thus, colored interactive images and video clips seem to catch our attention far better than a plain text. After all, there is a reason for the dramatic popularity of videos and video games. A judicious mix of visual and textual information might well serve the developmental needs of those with various learning styles.

VIDEO CONFERENCING

Video conferencing (e.g., ClassLivePro) is used to establish a simultaneous visual presence of the people dispersed in various geographic locations. It allows a group of people to communicate using both visual and audio means which promotes discussions, presentations, brainstorming and other collective activities.

It can be effective in online learning where you can set up a meeting or a discussion with a class in a different school, or with another institution, organization or a business related to the topic you study that will bring reality to the classroom.

Designing an Elementary Classroom

Learning takes place in a learning environment, which is commonly a classroom. The first thing in setting up an environment where learners can become actively engaged is to organize tables and chairs strategically to allow for flexible grouping. To learn by doing, the physical environment must be set up for social interaction. The key idea is to match structure and function. Since most classrooms are multipurpose, different seating arrangements in different parts of the room should offer your students different learning options. Although a part of your room could be set up for independent study, students need seating arrangements that enhance group activities.

> *The great aim of education is not knowledge but action.*
> Herbert Spencer (1820–1903)

Support for the notion that social interaction creates a learning environment is found in the writings of educational psychologists from Vygotsky to Slavin who have indicated that learning takes place within a social context that engenders meaningful interaction. Let's consider Vygotsky's notion of a zone of proximal development. This zone is premised on what a learner can do alone and what that same learner can do only with others. When setting up a classroom a seating arrangement should optimize sight lines (e.g. sitting in a circle) for a focused conversation where learners discuss important ideas stemming from their personal experiences while making explicit connections back to the text. These kinds of discussions clearly are facilitated by the students sitting in a circle on a carpet in a specially assigned part of the classroom or around tables (Fig 5.8), or a single round table (Fig 5.9), and are in concert with Vygotsky's notion that language is a primary vehicle for communicating ideas and enhancing intellectual development.

Although focused group conversations are an essential part of the daily activities in your classroom, other physical learning environments must be created to best serve all the different tasks students must perform (Fig. 5.8). Such spatial planning can accommodate special education students, EL students studying ESL, like-readiness learners, mixed-readiness groups, learners of similar interests, learners of different interests and peer-tutors who act as role models.

Even in a traditional rectangular classroom, you can create many nooks and crannies by using shelving and lightweight partitioning to transform various spaces into resource areas. Creative room arrangements allow students to experience learning in a multiplicity of contexts and can enhance performance in an array of developmental tasks.

A key outcome of a multipurpose elementary classroom design is that as students work in this environment they develop a sense of "site know-how". Understanding where to go in the room to have a

● **FIGURE 5.8 Design of an Elementary Classroom**

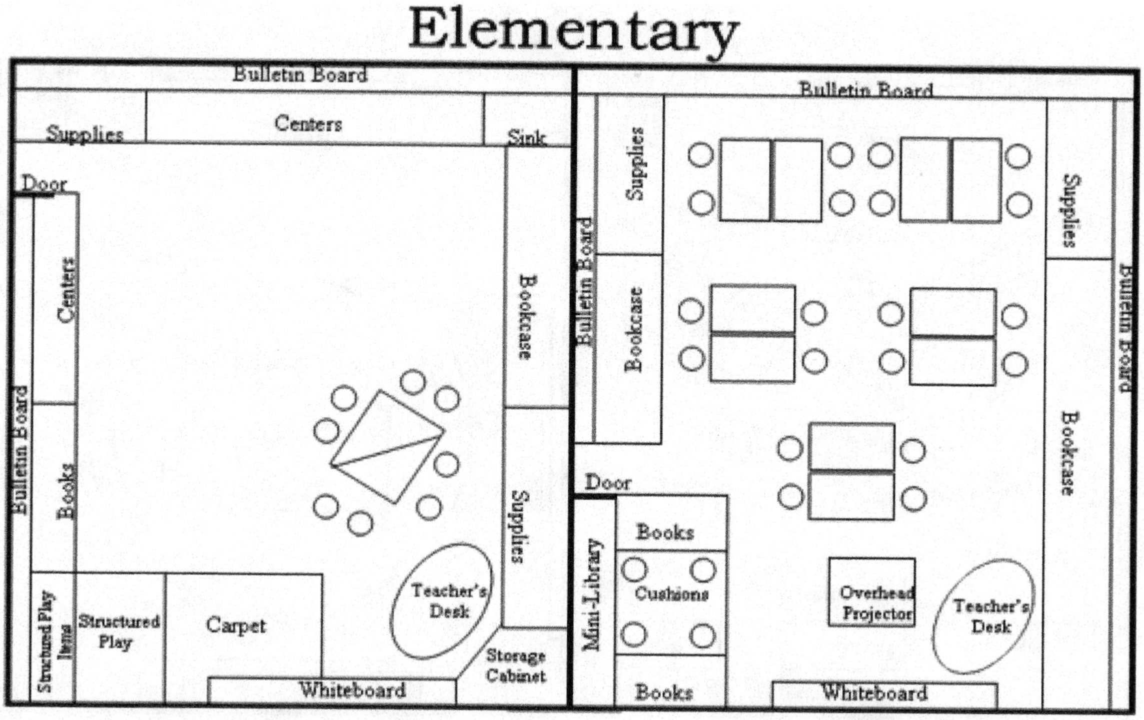

Elementary

different kind of learning experience and knowing how to interact with a wide variety of students makes for a learning environment that bolsters both academic development and social growth.

Designing a Secondary Classroom

Compared to elementary school, the secondary school has a distinct format where disciplines are divided into different classrooms. For example, when the classroom is constructed for learning science at the secondary level, the focus and function is not on merely reading or learning about, for instance chemistry, but a more hands-on approach—doing chemistry. With an emphasis on experimentation, time (i.e. extended lab periods) and space (e.g. worktables) are built in for the collection, discussion and analysis of data. An adequately designed science classroom should set an atmosphere where small and large groups of students can meet to inquire, plan, conduct investigations and think critically, constructing both explanations and scientific arguments.

● **FIGURE 5.9   Design of a High School Classroom**

High School

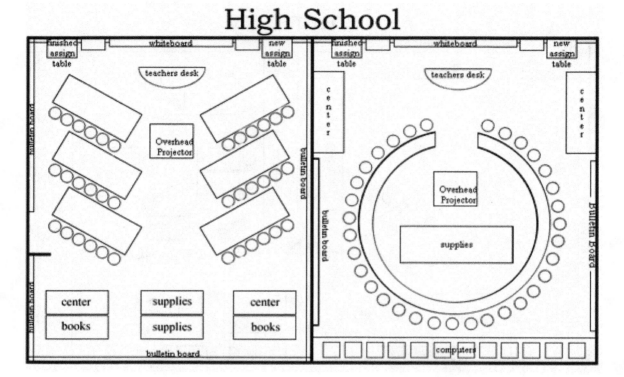

Interactive classrooms positively affect focused communication. A structurally interactive classroom is a model where seating arrangements promote scholarly discourse and expose students to a variety of academic and societal concerns.

Simply put, structure enhances function. Clearly a classroom set up for science (with an equipped lab), for journalism (with access to computers and phones), or for drama (with a stage) are secondary school physical environments that enhance the learning of a specific discipline (Fig. 5.9).

In either elementary or secondary classrooms both group and individual workspaces are provided to meet the needs of students with different learning styles who may be at different stages of academic and/or social development. In short, the physical environment can truly impact learning.

Thus, the way you teach a class is clearly affected by the classroom environment and seating arrangement you use. For example, a cooperative approach needs to have a flexible seating model—seating clusters to implement strategies for organizing teams or group learning activities across and within grade levels. The use of space also has an effect on the efficient use of time. Different activities where students are learning different things at the same time can take place in the same classroom if proper space provisions are made. For instance, some students can read silently wearing headphones to block out sound, while others can view a DVD of Shakespeare's *Henry V* in stereo.

Given your thoughtful classroom design, students have an optimal environment in which to demonstrate their skills and knowledge at the highest level of competence and efficiency. Remember to set up your "model" classroom to reflect the kinds of learning options and alternatives you wish to present to the students.

Another important addition to the classroom is instructional tools and materials used to create real-life environment via visuals (demonstrating slides or video clips when teaching about the environment, transport, travel, culture, shops and restaurants), realia and manipulatives (actual objects used in teaching, such as price lists from the stores, menus from the restaurants, fashion magazines, toy telephones, dishes and furniture). For instance, when in an ESL or French lesson you teach students to order food at the restaurant in the target language, you can show slides with the restaurant, or a video clip at the restaurant, give students menus and invite them to order food in the role play where one of the students is a patron while another is a waiter.

With so many resource options and alternatives in our quill, it is time now to move to understand the types of procedures to be used in the lesson plan. How we learn to a great extent determines what we learn. Accordingly, what procedures we follow as teachers can open or close the gateway to knowledge for many of our students. Chapter 6 will demonstrate effective procedures you can use in your classroom and beyond.

CHAPTER 6

Lesson Procedures

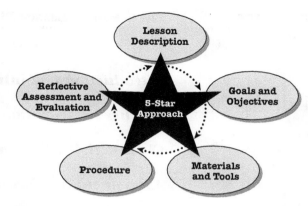

First Iteration

Like a music conductor, the teacher must lead an orchestra according to a set plan. There are many strategies and various ways to present a lesson plan and engage students in learning, but it is the teacher who must decide on how new material is to be presented and implemented so that every student participates in an active learning environment.

Lesson procedure is the function of the lesson plan. When implemented in the classroom, the procedure usually runs in five major activities: introduction, new material presentation, activities, assessment/evaluation, and closure.

Each lesson develops as a procedure within a preset time period. This procedure is filled with various activities, both teacher's and students'. First of all, the teacher starts a lesson introducing students into the new lesson, explaining the lesson's topic, its goal, objectives and planned learning outcomes. Then the teacher may present the new material, after which students will engage in different organized activities in which they develop deep understanding of the new knowledge and corresponding skills in using this knowledge. Finally, the teacher assesses and evaluates students' performance, and sums up the lesson outcomes in a closure. This is a typical lesson procedure which, however, may change according to the curriculum, lesson design and specific conditions of the today's lesson. The procedure is determined by the lesson's goal, objectives, learning outcomes and content.

Introduction (. . . min.): _____

Teacher presentation (. . . min.): The teacher will: _____

Class activities (. . . min.): Students will: _____

Assessment and Evaluation (min.): _____

Closure (. . . min.): _____

In the 2nd and 3rd iterations of this chapter we will analyze various procedures addressing teacher's and students' activities.

Second Iteration

This iteration will analyze various procedures, strategies and activities you will use in the lesson you are going to teach.

A lesson is an organized and timed procedure filled with various activities intended for students' learning new things. Each of the activities is a procedure in itself. Let's consider all these procedures.

Overview of Procedures

Introduction (. . . min.): _____

_____

_____

Teacher Presentation (. . . min.): **The teacher will:**

_____

_____

Class Activities (. . . min.): **Students will:**

_____

_____

Assessment and Evaluation (. . . min.): _____

_____

_____

Closure (. . . min.): _____

_____

_____

Coming to Terms Over Procedure

The 5-Minute Lesson Plan consists of five major components: lesson description, goals and objectives, materials and tools, procedure, and finally assessment and evaluation. While lesson description contains general information about the lesson, such as lesson topic, grade, class characteristics (how many students, how many special education and ELL students, etc.), goals, objectives, learning outcomes, and standards, a critical part of any lesson is the **procedure** where the teacher and students interact and communicate, engage with the lesson's content and with each other, share information, solve problems and do assignments to achieve the lesson's goals and objectives and produce the planned learning outcomes. It is through activities that knowledge is constructed and retained, and skills are developed and applied. The teacher assesses and evaluates student performance and outcomes of these activities.

The ***5-Minute Lesson Plan*** is implemented in 5 major steps (Fig 6.1). Student activities are, by far, the most important part of the procedure. Hence you should focus your attention on making them engaging and effective. A crucial factor of effective lesson planning which affects its implementation is the timing of all these steps, the question being how long you and your students should be engaged in a particular activity? Timing like mortar holds the lesson structure

● **FIGURE 6.1   Lesson Plan Structure**

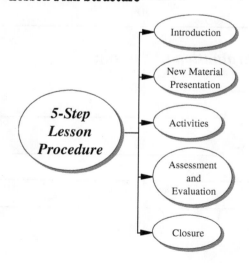

together. You will allocate the time based on lesson goal and objectives, volume of new knowledge, your experience, and class variables, including student capabilities, background knowledge and skills. It is convenient to write the time near each activity in minutes, for example, group discussion of the topic—10 minutes

Types of Procedures

There are various types of procedures, and their application is determined by the goals and objectives of a particular lesson. Lesson plan development, of course, depends on the types of procedures used. While procedures can been defined conceptually, they almost always are implemented in combination. Here are different of procedures which are typically found mixed and matched as a lesson plan dictates (Fig. 6.2):

1. New content presentation
2. Student activities
3. Student practice
4. Field work
5. Review

There are also other procedures that are commonly used in the lesson, such as introduction, homework checkup, new home assignment, and closure.

In preparing a lesson plan, you decide which of the procedures or combination of procedures you need to use to meet the lesson objectives.

● **FIGURE 6.2   Lesson Procedures**

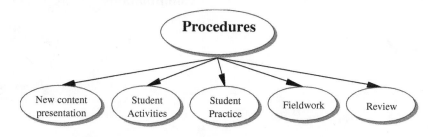

● WHAT'S THE PLAN?

As you start developing a procedure, decide on how you might carry it out. (**Hint:** *Think of the various procedures or combination of procedures you should select from in order to achieve the objectives.*)

_____

_____

_____

_____

A lesson may be wholly devoted to one type of procedure, e.g. student activities or evaluation (test); however, more often a practical lesson is a combination of several types of procedures. The choice depends on the lesson goals, objectives, lesson content and plan, environment, and students' characteristics (e.g. responsiveness to today's class needs). Some typical procedural combinations are (Fig 6.3):

- Review + new material presentation
- New material presentation + activities

● FIGURE 6.3   Lesson Procedure Combinations

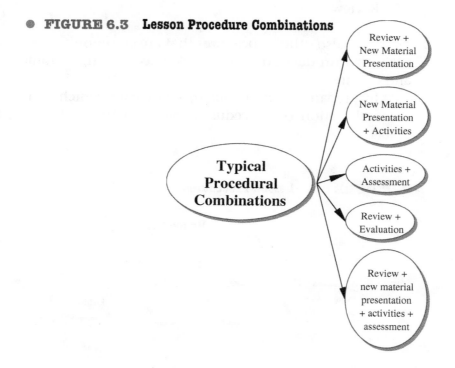

- Activities + assessment
- Review + evaluation
- Review + new material presentation + activities + assessment

New Material Presentation Module and its Implementation

New material presentation speaks for itself—it is actually an introduction of the new content. It may include the following basic activities (Fig 6.4):

- Question and answer session (it has two variations: teacher posing a question and then answering it, or teacher asking students to answer the question and then commenting)
- Teacher lecture and/or demonstration
- Student presentation(s) based on previously given assignment
- Class or independent reading of the text
- Technology-based presentation (e.g. using PowerPoint, video, or multimedia) together with the teacher's lecture or commentaries, or without the teacher's direct participation (e.g. showing a movie)
- Invited speaker presentation

Recall that lecture is the least effective way of teaching because it is not engaging the students.

● **FIGURE 6.4 New Material Presentation**

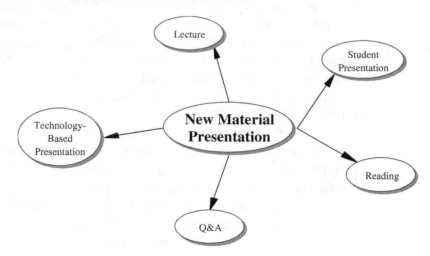

● **WHAT'S THE PLAN?**

To prepare a presentation of the new material, you should decide what content to present, and how you are going to communicate. (**Hint:** *Think of the various presentation modes you might select from for the content to be effectively acquired, understood and retained by your students.*)

_____

_____

_____

_____

Activities and Practice

Lesson procedure is focused on developing student understanding of the material, building new knowledge, creating concepts, developing appropriate skills, and constructing personal meaning. The activities selected for the procedure reflect your methodological approach which, to be most effective, should be geared to your students' learning styles.

Apply learner-centered approaches; reality-based, situated learning; problem-solving; case studies; role playing; service learning; team or small group work and other collaborative activities. Utilize your students' prior knowledge which may be found in their authentic personal experiences.

Procedure includes both teacher instructional activities and student learning activities. The former embraces presentation strategies described above, setting tasks and assignments, prompting students' participation and engagement, facilitating implementation of the learning tasks, using various motivational factors, and supporting student learning. The latter activities may be of at least two levels of complexity: basic activities (guided learning events) and advanced activities (independent practice).

The difference between these levels is as follows: basic activities are to be accomplished according to selected patterns or simple models, with little flexibility in their implementation and under the direction of the teacher. This is done because the objective here is to build primary knowledge and develop initial skills, following a certain sample and using particular limited information. First level activities include Q&A, reading, mnemonic exercises and drills, peer collaboration based on imitation, problem-solving, role playing and educational games (Fig 6.5).

● **FIGURE 6.5   Basic Student Activities**

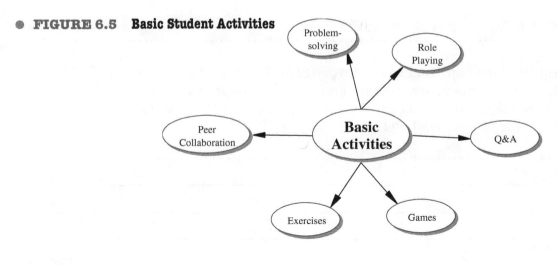

● **FIGURE 6.6   Advanced Student Activities**

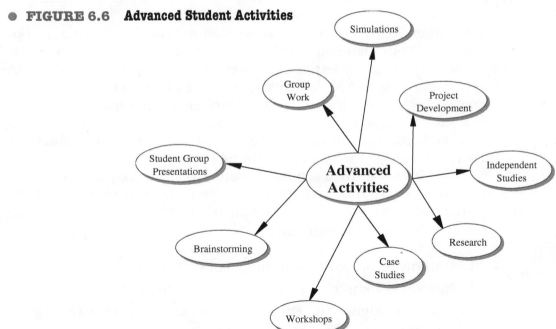

In teaching English language learners, you may include various language exercises, such as drills, Close testing, substitution, multiple choice, and simple communicative exercises, such as simulation and role playing.

Advanced activities defined as independent practice represent application of the recently learned material and skills in new situations, for example, in a case study, dramatization or lab experiment. So, independent practice activities can include: case studies, group work, workshops, independent studies, brainstorming, simulations, research, project development and student group presentations. (Fig 6.6).

● WHAT'S THE PLAN?

To help students construct new knowledge and develop new skills, decide on what procedures you are going to use. (**Hint:** *Think of the various procedures you should select for students to effectively understand, retain and use new material and new skills.)*

_____

_____

_____

_____

_____

What, then, is a **structured classroom activity**? It is a major component of your plan and a basic unit of organized learning. Of course, an activity within a lesson plan may be also a model of knowledge application in practice. When you teach ELs how to communicate in English, you teach them to do it through communicative exercises that imitate real communication. You set realistic communicative tasks and create circumstances that would simulate real-life situations. Then you engage the EL in performing these tasks.

For instance, in teaching students to make acquaintances you first demonstrate how you introduce yourself, and then model this activity with one of the more advanced students. Then you give the class the following assignments:

1. Introduce yourself to your neighbor on the left.
2. Introduce yourself to your neighbor on the right.
3. Ask your neighbor on the right to introduce you to your neighbor on the left.
4. Introduce your neighbor on the left to your neighbor on the right.
5. Introduce yourself to the class.
6. Ask your neighbor on the right about your neighbor on the left.
7. Ask your neighbor on the left about other people in the class.

8. You are at a reception. Try to meet as many people as you can. Don't forget to introduce yourself each time you meet other people.

9. Make up a list of all those present in the room.

In this simulated activity students will be trying to achieve their pragmatic communicative goals in actual conversation in the target language. The objectives are not simply to memorize new words and patterns (mere information), but to engage the learners in meaningful person-to-person interactions (procedures leading to skill development). This is how second or foreign language communicative skills should be developed.

When you give your students assignments in the classroom, see that these assignments are meaningfully related to the students' background and potential application in real life. For instance, if you want your students talk about food, you can set an atmosphere where students express genuine interest in doing a particular assignment by suggesting they are hungry and you are going to take them to a (virtual) restaurant. Show them a video clip about a restaurant, or a couple of slides showing restaurant views, give them several menus from the restaurants, and suggest that they order food according to their liking. If you role play, breaking the class into pairs where one student will play the role of a customer, and the other will be a waiter, will create a fun activity with very effective outcomes.

● WHAT'S THE PLAN?

As you think about lesson plan strategies and activities, what, in your opinion, is the difference between transmitting information and engaging students in a meaning- centered activity? (**Hint:** *Think of the distinction between mere information and meaning—which do you think better engages the student?*)

_____

_____

_____

_____

● **FIGURE 6.7   Homework Checkup**

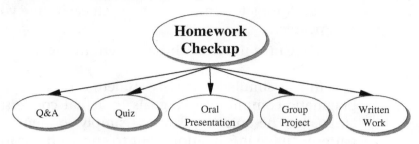

Homework Checking Module and its Implementation

To check students' homework is important not only to regulate student preparation for the class, but also to reinforce the material for better retention and validate the students' independent work. Homework checkup can include such activities as (Fig 6.7):

- Question and answer session
- Quiz on homework
- Written work submission
- Students' oral presentation
- Group project presentation

● WHAT'S THE PLAN?

To review students' homework, decide on what activities you are going to use. (**Hint:** *Think of the various activities you should select for student work to be effectively presented, validated and retained.*)

_____

_____

_____

_____

_____

Final Thoughts

Recall, the difference between school subject disciplines is not only in the content but also in the conceptual flow of the class. Methodologically speaking, a given course (science, math, drama) may call into use different cognitive processes that require distinct activities. The lessons in these classes may have similar structure but differ in content, concepts and instructional strategies. This means that you may have to develop a specific set of strategies, activities, assignments, assessment tools and techniques for each discipline you teach.

● WHAT'S THE PLAN?

Recall what is the function of each component:

Introduction: _____

_____

Homework Checkup: _____

_____

Teacher Presentation: _____

_____

Accommodations for ELs: _____

_____

Student Activities: _____

_____

Assessment and Evaluation: _____

_____

Closure: _____

_____

Your Turn—Practice Sheets

I. PROCEDURE

Note: Now it is your turn to practice writing out the procedure portion of the lesson plan. Do five examples. Think of the block of time you have to teach a lesson and then approximate how long you will need (in minutes) to complete each of the six steps in the procedure section.

Introduction (. . . min.): _____

_____

_____

Homework Checkup (. . . min.): _____

_____

_____

Teacher Presentation (. . . min.): _____

_____

_____

Assessment and Evaluation (. . . min.): _____

_____

_____

Homework: _____

_____

_____

Closure (. . . min.): _____

_____

_____

Third Iteration

• •

This iteration will delve into important aspects of lesson planning and teaching, including strategies and activities, their types, and the way they may be organized in the lesson via an Iterative Instructional Model.

Overview of Procedure
• •

       Introduction (. . . min.): _____

       Teacher presentation (. . . min.): _____

       Class activities (. . . min.): _____

       Assessment and Evaluation (min.): _____

       Closure (. . . min.): _____

Coming to Terms Over Strategies and Activities
• •

Strategies are particular implementations of a method through specially organized instructional activities. There are strategies for teachers and students. Teacher strategies involve presenting carefully chosen instructional materials, organizing student collaborative and independent work, and managing the class. Student strategies are intended for learners to construct knowledge and develop skills. Student strategies can be for classroom and out-of-classroom use, as in homework, field activities and community service.

    Each strategy is used for a specific purpose. An instructional strategy has a practical purpose which should be meaningful to a student. Goals and objectives that emanate from a strategy connect learning with real life. On the other hand, an objective states a specific instructional aim of an activity that is to be evaluated. While goals are general in scope, objectives are specific and quantifiable. This allows you to establish if the goal has been met, objectives reached and learning outcomes achieved through evaluation at the end of the lesson.

It is important to understand the implicit hierarchy of certain pedagogical terms in order to best understand where strategies fit in the overall design of the lesson plan. Consider the following:

A **method** is a theoretical instructional approach. For example, one can practice the communicative approach, accelerated learning, or cooperative learning approaches. All are considered methodological in nature.

A **strategy,** as we have seen, is a particular implementation of a method through a specially organized instructional activity. For example, reading strategies include, among others, oral reading or sustained silent reading. A student might employ the notion of an outline as a writing strategy to prepare for an essay or a project. Skillful use of an outline can make the final product, the paper itself, a reflection of a clear, concise and coherent message.

An **activity** implements a strategy. A strategy in action is an activity. For instance, listening, speaking, reading, writing, dancing and singing can all be activities that forward a given conceptual strategy. Reciting a poem, writing an outline of a story, solving a problem or engaging in a dialogue on a topic are examples of activities.

An **instructional tool** is an instrument that facilitates teaching and learning. We know that forks or chopsticks are tools for eating. A book, a handout with a text, a magic marker, a transparency, a computer, or software program are all examples of instructional tools.

With these definitions in mind, we can make statements about specific goals and objectives for strategies that relate to fundamental descriptions of lesson plan goals and objectives which produce the planned outcomes (see Chapter 4).

Example of a strategy goal: We need to understand the effects of global warming.

Example of strategy objectives: Students will better understand the effects of global warming as they:

- Search, select, evaluate and process new information
- Disseminated new information in written reports
- Identify five effects of global warming cited in scientific literature
- Take part in a class roundtable to discuss their findings and come up with a proposed set of solutions

● WHAT'S THE PLAN?

Select five best strategies for a particular objective:

_____

_____

_____

_____

_____

Example of strategy goal: Students will identify good eating habits through a dialogue on food preparation and consumption.

Example of strategy objectives: Students will learn and use the new vocabulary while preparing a delicious salad as they:

- Learn to say, spell and read the words lettuce, walnuts, raisins, vinegar, olive oil, salad bowl, forks, and plates
- Prepare a Greek salad
- Consume the salad
- Take part in a short student-to-student dialog about the experience (This can be used by both ELL and English-speaking students.)

● WHAT'S THE PLAN?

Construct a set of five strategies and select two which you believe could be the most effective.

_____

_____

_____

_____

_____

Strategies are seldom used in isolation: usually it takes more than one methodological approach to ensure understanding of new material, concept formation, retention, and automated skill development. For instance, it was established that it takes multiple uses (dozen of times) of a new foreign word in various contexts (listening, saying aloud, reading, writing, using in speech) to assure its retention and flexible utilization in communication. Therefore, in a lesson, for a particular topic or theme, a concise and varied set of strategies and appropriate activities is typically developed. Teachers should base this set on the needs the affective and cognitive needs of their students. It can follow the Iterative Instructional Model, which will be described in this chapter.

An example: A topic based on textual information to be presented in the class may require four activities (Fig 6.8).

We know a **strategy** is the particular implementation of a method that operates through specially organized instructional activities. Let's look at these nine component parts that offer an effective structure you can use in your classroom. As you review the list, think of specific examples of each component to make your strategic decisions effective. An instructionally effective strategy that produces the planned outcome usually has the following nine components:

1. Goal
2. Objectives
3. Learning materials and tools necessary to achieve the goal and objectives within a given task, topic or content
4. A role an individual student will play in this activity
5. Group role characteristics for each participant of the activity, when it is a collaborative one
6. Genuine student motivation to effectively accomplish the activity
7. An appropriate physical or virtual environment that makes up the situation for the activity (simulating real-life circumstances)
8. An outline of the procedure for achieving the planned outcomes (plan of action)
9. Time for implementation.

● **FIGURE 6.8   Topic**

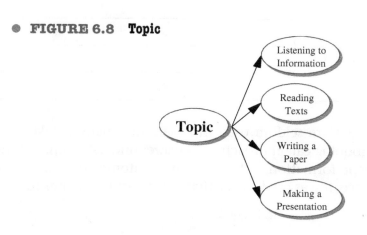

Let's think in terms of a strategy. Imagine you have just been named to coach the football team! You are excited at the opportunity but at the same time realize that to be a successful coach you must employ a **strategy** by putting into practice a method that you will carry out in your specially organized activities on the practice field. You **goal** is to win football games. Your **objectives** are to teach the fundamentals of the game so your players will learn and refine various psychomotor activities: how to block, tackle, run with the ball, throw the ball and catch the ball. You devise **learning materials** that make up your playbook comprised of set plays to achieve your goals by means of successfully demonstrating the objectives, and tools (a ball, diagrams, videos). **Individual students roles** are based on your selection taking into consideration where students feel they can contribute at the various positions (e.g. you need to designate linemen, linebackers, backs and kickers). **Group role characteristics** are critical because in order for the team to function at its best the needs of the team trump individual wants.

Genuine student motivation is present when the coach sets an environment where members of the team choose to do their best on the field of play. Recall in football as in life it is the affective domain (values and emotions) that trigger the cognitive domain (thought) and spur psychomotor activity (physical action). The **appropriate physical or virtual environment** takes place on the gridiron or the classroom in order to study video clips of the team's practice or your opponents' games. Your **outline of the procedure for achieving planned outcomes** is inserted into you game plan. Finally the **time for implementation** is game day! In the next 60 minutes you and your team will face the ultimate evaluation—the scoreboard. The outcome will be winning the game and quality of each player's performance. As the season proceeds you will have time for reflective assessment to continually work to improve your team's performance based on the various strategies you employ.

● WHAT'S THE PLAN?

Write your two favorite strategies for second language development.
Identify nine components for each strategy.

_____

_____

_____

_____

_____

Student learning is the ***raison d'être*** for teaching. Learner-centered approaches require that teachers facilitate student learning by setting an environment where the main focus in the lesson plan is on promoting <u>student</u> engagement. While the goals and objectives for the student and the teacher may well differ, successful outcomes for the learner remain paramount. For example, students might be geared to practical and realistic endeavors to solve a problem and complete a task. On the other hand, teachers are attempting to set up a lesson plan where students master the new material and develop specific skills. Accordingly, it is the student who plays an active part in most of the activities—not the teacher. Novice teachers tend to lecture and explain ideas and skills themselves which results in a passive and ineffective learning experience for the student.

With a well-constructed lesson plan, however, active student engagement in learning is promoted due to a superior learning design where the learner chooses to more fully participate in his or her own educational experience. Therefore students should be given assignments, materials, tools and *time* to do the job themselves and stay effectively engaged. That is why a lesson plan has to contain a sufficient number of student activities to ensure knowledge construction and development of planned skills, while the teacher's work is to set the goals, objectives, and outline the outcomes, and to create the most enriching and stress-free environment for student learning activities.

There are different ways to classify strategies: by content area, by grade, by activities, (e.g., teacher or student activities; classroom or out-of-class activities; individual or group activities; reading, writing, communication, and problem-solving activities, role playing and discussion). We offer a model based on the ***5-Star Lesson*** plan structure: introduction, presentation, student activities (basic and advanced), closure, homework (extension of learning), and community-based activities.

● WHAT'S THE PLAN?

Write your five favorite strategies for math (reading, second language) skill development:

_____

_____

_____

_____

_____

Strategies

READING

1. Use the text to find information about...; present your findings
2. Write a short summary of the text
3. Write a plan of the text
4. Answer questions on the text
5. Prepare an essay describing a particular issue discussed in the text
6. Use the text to write the continuation of the story
7. Compare issues covered in two texts
8. Describe a character or a situation
9. Analyze and critically assess a particular situation in the text
10. Offer your opinion on the situation described in the text
11. Prepare a to discuss the meaning of the text
12. Write a critical analysis of the text

INFORMATION SEARCH

1. Find information on a particular topic
2. Collect information on a particular topic from three different sources; compare and assess information from all three sources
3. Describe various ways of gathering information and offer your suggestions for the most efficient collection techniques.

OBSERVATION

1. Look at the picture: what do you want to say about it? What is the most striking in it?
2. Observe the person or a group of people engaged in a particular work and describe their behaviors
3. Watch a carpenter's (gardener's, teacher's) work and write an essay about it.
4. Watch a news program: what is the major news of today?

● WHAT'S THE PLAN?

Write your five favorite strategies for reading development:

_____

_____

_____

_____

_____

CONSTRUCTION

1. Make up an automobile from Lego parts and describe the process and the outcome.
2. Build a model house and explain how you did it.
3. Assemble words from letter blocks

WRITING

1. Write a letter to your parents about your trip to the zoo or your community work
2. Write a letter to your friend about your new toys or a book
3. Write a diary about your summer vacation
4. Write a story about your friend's adventure
5. Interview your grandparents about a major event in their life and write a report

DRAWING

1. Draw a floor plan of your house
2. Draw a picture based on your favorite story (fairy tale)
3. Draw your toys
4. Draw a picture from the street or a park

LISTENING

1. Listen to a prerecorded text and repeat words imitating the sounds after the speaker
2. Listen to a story on tape or DVD and tell the class about it

3. Listen to a radio broadcast and write a short report
4. Watch a movie and discuss what the actors spoke about.

DEVELOPING COMMUNICATION SKILLS IN A SECOND LANGUAGE

1. Ask and answer questions
2. Conduct a dialogue on the topic
3. Engage in role playing modeling real-life situation
4. Hold a thematic discussion

SOLVING LIFE'S PROBLEMS

1. Here is a problem we have in school...; offer your solution.
2. You want to buy a new computer game. It costs $80. You have only $55. What are you going to do?
3. Your parents do not allow you to visit your friend's house. Try to convince them to permit the visit.
4. You don't know how to write an essay on the topic. Analyze your shortcomings and identify the plan of actions.
5. Your friend has a problem understanding chemical reactions. Try to help him.

CALCULATING

1. Calculate how much your family spends on food per month
2. If you want to walk from your home to school, how long will it take you to get there? (Divide the distance by your speed.)

● WHAT'S THE PLAN?

Write your five favorite strategies for writing development:

_____

_____

_____

_____

_____

Activities

Here is a short list of major activities you can use in the lesson.

INTRODUCTION

1. Teacher reviewing previous topic
2. Teacher asking questions on the previously learned material
3. Having a student or two review the previous topic
4. Having a few students ask questions on major issues of the previous material and others respond
5. Demonstrating some visuals related to the previous topic and asking students to elaborate
6. Running a short informal review (preferably oral) with questions on the previous topic and then discussing it with the class

NEW MATERIAL PRESENTATION

1. Teacher giving a lecture or a demonstration (accompanied by visuals, video clips or PowerPoint presentation) and engaging students in the discussion by asking questions at certain points
2. Selected students making prepared presentation on the new topic
3. Having a guest teacher or presenter speak on a new topic
4. Demonstrating a video (educational movie) or multimedia presentation and commenting
5. Having students search for new information in the texts, online or in real-life situations (before or during the lesson) and present it to the class

STUDENT ACTIVITIES:

Individual

1. Reading a text for meaning
2. Searching for information in printed or electronic sources
3. Observing an object or process (watching a demonstration, an experiment, a real-life situation or a video clip)
4. Interviewing
5. Constructing or producing an object from parts (Lego, clay figure, maze)

6. Writing a paper (essay)
7. Drawing a picture or a chart
8. Listening (to somebody or to a radio, or a recording)
9. Solving a problem
10. Calculating
11. Designing
12. Planning
13. Mimicking or posing (pantomime)
14. Playing a game
15. Presenting or demonstrating
16. Doing physical work or exercise
17. Memorizing
18. Singing
19. Reciting
20. Preparing to participate in a dialogue, in a group discussion or a presentation (including brainstorming)
21. Making a speech

Group (team work, collaboration or cooperation)—pair work, small group (3–4 students), large group (5 or more), half and full class.

1. Discussing
2. Exchanging information
3. Developing a project
4. Performing a joint activity
5. Solving a problem
6. Playing a game
7. Role playing
8. Dramatizing
9. Competing
10. Brainstorming
11. Singing
12. Presenting to a group with a subsequent discussion
13. Going an excursion or a tour
14. Participating in a community project

Depending on the size of the group the dynamics of each of these activities will change. For instance, pair work is great for conducting a dialogue or producing a joint work; a small group (3–4 students) is effective for collaboration and cooperation on a problem or project; a larger group (5 or more students) can be used for group discussion or presentation of team or individual projects.

These lists are a starting points for activities you can expand to best meet the needs of all of your students.

ASSESSMENT AND EVALUATION

1. Observing students' work
2. Making individual comments
3. Having a teacher-student conference after the lesson
4. Offering a quiz, test or exam
5. Reviewing students' written assignments
6. Suggesting that students write a self-evaluation or a reflection paper
7. Peer-editing or commenting on other student's work

CLOSURE

1. Teacher reviewing the lesson's main points
2. Students reviewing the lesson's main points
3. Teacher asking questions on the new material
4. Teacher discussing student performance and praising them

Homework/Extension and Community-Based Activities

Homework activities extend classroom learning and are intended for ensuring student retention, knowledge construction, skill development and independent thinking. They cannot just be reading or writing assignments based on the textbook but activities requiring the student's autonomous and creative work focused on real-life situation in the family, the community, the nation and the world.

Some examples are interviewing people on different topics, creating and running a survey, observing and discussing various environmental and social problems, developing projects, making some objects, participating in community activities and reporting them.

This list of activities can be certainly expanded. Selection of activities in the lesson planning stage, their organization in the lesson, and their implementation depend on selected strategies that are set to meet the lesson goals and objectives. A teacher develops a strategy focusing on specific goals and objectives that allow students to achieve successful learning outcomes embedded in the lesson plan. A teacher then sets an environment based on an enriched curriculum, a wide variety of methodological approaches, strategies and tools so that students choose to be motivated, engaged, and ultimately empowered.

● WHAT'S THE PLAN?

How would you present the same content in five different ways?
(**Hint:** *Use different modalities, such as lecturing, reading a text, listening to a recording, viewing a PowerPoint presentation or a video clip):*

_____

_____

_____

_____

_____

An Iterative Instructional Model

Let's discuss two models of the learning process: a linear (sequential) model, and an iterative (spiral). Ordinarily, the lesson structure is linear, that is, developing from one step to another (Fig 6.9):

A generic lesson plan model is an example of a linear structure. All the activities in the lesson follow one another. Yet, in real learning we usually need to address the same content and skills more than once in order to ensure better understanding and retention.

Instruction generally starts with an elementary acknowledgment of the fact that repeated practice is a universal method of learning. *Repetitio est mater studiorum*, says the old Latin proverb. Repetition inherently includes several learning cycles, reiterating or reusing the same content or the same set of instructional activities. For example, to master spelling, one repeats the letters of the word neighbor n-e-i-g-h-b-o-r five times to "embed" the knowledge. One can then self-assess,

● **FIGURE 6.9   Linear Instructional Model**

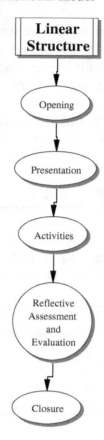

by closing one's eyes so not to look at the spelling word and then repeat the letters in the correct order.

There can also be repetitive, cyclic activities in some stages of a lesson (Fig. 6.10).

For instance, in the presentation phase a teacher can make a short lecture (Presentation 1) then demonstrate a video on the same topic (Presentation 2), and then suggest that students independently find additional information on the topic on the Internet or in the available books (Presentation 3), thus providing a diversified, multimodal introduction of the new information. In the activities phase, to ensure better knowledge construction and skill development, various strategies should be applied targeting the same content and same skills.

Another example, if students are working on reading, one of the activities (1) can be chorus reading, another (2) could be silent individual reading, and third (3), might be small group discussion of the items found in the text. This approach guarantees better understanding of information, effective knowledge construction, longer retention, and stronger skills.

● **FIGURE 6.10   Cyclic Learning Structure**

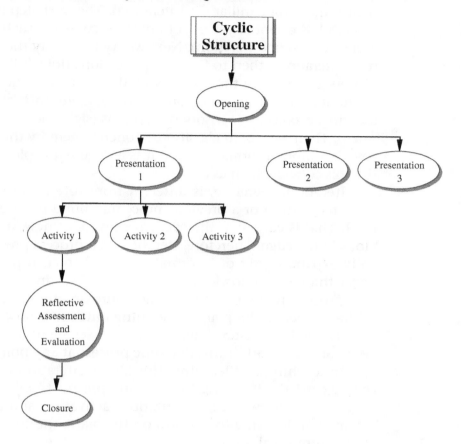

● **WHAT'S THE PLAN?**

How would you diversify the student learning process with the same content in five different ways? (**Hint:** *Use varied activities that involve individual, pair, small group and full class work, and apply technology-based strategies*):

_____

_____

_____

_____

_____

The iterative, or cyclic format (cyclic learning) is a natural way to acquire knowledge. We discover the world iteratively, that is to say, in cycles. Being confronted with a new abstract concept, we try to discover at first the main information about the object in order to identify it with something familiar (first iteration). The next step is to analyze the object's less essential yet important characteristics, such as form, shape, and color (second iteration). Next we try to classify these characteristics (third iteration), then to find its applications (fourth iteration), and the process goes on. On the other hand, the iterative model adapts to a different sequence when the concept is concrete. In that case we would identify an object by sensory perceptions (sight, hearing, taste, touch or smell). Then we would classify the concrete item by thinking about discovering more information (e.g. it is a large red apple) and finally classify this concrete item as a fruit.

Iteration, therefore, is different from rote drill in that it is not a mere replication of a previous procedure but a recurrence at a higher level. That is each step the cyclic process adds new knowledge to previous knowledge. Therefore, iteration as a process presupposes a gradually expanding set of information added to each preceding cycle to boost the initial knowledge and increase learning within each cycle. This process at any point marks an approximation of the current state of the learner to the planned learning outcome as he or she moves to an increased understanding. Reflective assessment and evaluation can be an ongoing part of this dynamic process at any point.

In teaching and learning, this kind of iteration is a repeated procedure carried out during the learning process to provide cyclic levels of increased knowledge presentation, activation and application. For example, in learning to perform on the piano the student is presented with the musical score, and actively strikes the keys in order to produce the music. The consistent application of practice can over time produce not only a more a more refined musical rendition but increase the student's appreciation and, via motor skills, presentation of the piece. The same principle applies to developing communicative skills in a target language, which requires numerous iterations of the same material in various contexts and situations.

Each cycle contains a model of the whole content area approximated to a given level of knowledge. Each subsequent cycle is based on the preceding one and adds to it some details thus bringing more extended and a deeper understanding. Learning starts with the first iteration that presents the whole topic but at first only on an introductory level, without specific details, just major concepts, relationships, and an overall structure. Each subsequent iteration adds new details to the initial presentation thus increasing its complexity and coverage, until the topic is exhausted. The final iteration is reflective in nature, offering an overview of the topic, recapitulating its principal points.

Therefore, iteration can serve as a mechanism for knowledge construction and management, for improving retention of knowledge, and for effective skill development. The basic idea behind the Iterative Instructional Model is that the learner should learn from previous cycles, expand his or her knowledge and perform better at every new cycle. Learning actually takes place in a set of iterations. (The principle of cycle repetition of activities is used in the Iterative Instructional Model (Greiner, Serdyukov et al. 2005).

The idea of recurrence or repetition is not new. What is different about our approach is the recognition of the organization of the whole learning process as a system of cycles that occur in all stages of the learning process. They be can found at all levels of the curriculum design, the program, the content area, the unit, and the lesson.

The following are a few examples of the cycles:

Cycle 1. A curricular program contains elements that are interrelated and interdependent; in the beginning of a one's program students are given its overview.

Cycle 2. Each discipline starts with the introduction previewing its structure, content, activities and outcomes.

Cycle 3. The specific course is concluded with a reflective general review, highlighting its most essential issues.

Cycle 4. Every lesson begins with the preview of the new plan and ends with the reflective review of the most important items.

These cycles are repetitive in nature.

● WHAT'S THE PLAN?

How can you apply an iterative approach in teaching your content area? (**Hint:** *Think of doing the same activity in five different ways*):

_____

_____

_____

_____

_____

_____

The interrelations between the learning modules and cycles are not vertical, rather they are built into a spiral: each lower level connected to and spiraling to the next higher level.

There are several significant implications to the Iterative Instructional Model. The cyclic approach helps to improve the structure and organization of the delivery of curriculum and of the students' learning. It provides a better conceptual understanding of the curricular content because it continuously supports the integral vision of the spiral. A *spiral curriculum* (J. Brunner) develops through revisiting foundational concepts repeatedly, constructing upon them new knowledge as the learner better understands the meaning and depth of what is being studied. This approach also allows demonstrating and applying the links between each topic of a course of study with other topics and with other courses in a program, thus developing interdisciplinary links.

Two or more cycles covering one topic may have a common practicum, student presentations, a video with a discussion, a visitor presentation with a subsequent student Q&A session or discussion, a story narration, a general discussion, and a text. This model can in many cases provide greater information retention and better skill development than a strictly linear approach.

Another example demonstrates the application of this model in a set of several cyclic activities each of which is focused on developing communicative ESL skills based on the same content (words and phrases)—see "Making Acquaintances" set of activities (Chapter 8). We are aware that a communicative skill develops through numerous applications of the same language material in cyclic communicative situations.

There are nine cyclic activities in this set, each similar to all the others in objective, content and process. The only difference between them is in changing tasks and communicative partners which provides for a highly motivated, non-monotonous and, consequently, varied repetitions of the same content in similar acts. Thus, this cyclic set ensures the necessary recurrence of the same activity in different circumstances for developing a sound skill and ensuring better retention of the designated language material without it necessarily becoming tedious.

To review, the overall process of knowledge construction based on Iterative Instructional Model connects each lower level activity to higher levels like a spiral. Its goal is gradual accumulation of knowledge in each of the cycles to an ever fuller representation. Each preceding cycle grows into the subsequent one, expanding the knowledge at each iteration. Each cycle represents a full model of the whole topic presented at a consecutively greater level of complexity, completeness and detail than the previous one (Fig. 6.11).

● **FIGURE 6.11**   **Iterative Instructional Process**

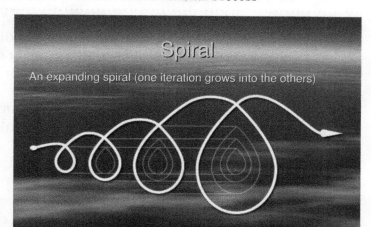

Iterative Instructional Model can be applied in the presentation phase where the content is cycled several times in different modalities (lecture, instructor demonstration, text, visuals, audio-visual or multi-media program and simulations). It is important in this cyclic structure that the topic is presented as a whole, in its entirety, though several increasing levels of presentation. In this way students perceive and process information a number of times in multiple formats which improves understanding and retention.

Iterative Instructional Model is particularly useful for effective knowledge construction and sound skill development. In the application phase where students demonstrate their new knowledge and skills in dealing with various life-based situations, this model helps to integrate new knowledge and skills in real-life situations.

● WHAT'S THE PLAN?

How would you explain the Iterative Instructional Model to your colleagues? (**Hint:** *Think of repetition, life cycles and other recurrent activities we use*):

_____

_____

_____

_____

_____

Final Thoughts and Terms

Recall, the difference between school subject disciplines is not only in the content but also in the conceptual flow of the class. Methodologically speaking, a given course (science, math, drama) may call into use different cognitive processes that require distinct activities. The lessons in these classes may have similar structure but differ in content, concepts and instructional strategies. This means that you may have to develop a specific set of strategies, activities, assignments, assessment tools and techniques for each discipline you teach.

Below is a framework for your lesson procedure. Please recall each component's function.

Introduction: _____

_____

Homework Checkup: _____

_____

Teacher Presentation: _____

_____

Accommodations for ELL/SDAIE: _____

_____

Student Activities: _____

_____

Assessment and Evaluation: _____

_____

Homework: _____

_____

Closure: _____

_____

To Sum Up

The **introduction** is the initial part or phase of the lesson intended to prepare students for learning by warming up, general conversation, reviewing the previous lesson's key points, setting the objectives and presenting the plan of the current lesson, and doing preliminary exercises. Here the rationale for the lesson is given, including the state content standards and the explanation of why the lesson is important for the learner. Goals and objectives have to be explained to the students so they know what they will be doing and why, and learning outcomes identified. In every lesson, the teacher should always make reference to what is being learned, why it is important for the student, and how it relates to other learning. Therefore, the learner should be aware of the relevance of a specific skill or a given activity. The general demeanor of a caring and competent teacher is essential at this stage of the lesson to lower the students' level of anxiety.

Homework checkup to be reviewed in class is a stage during which the students present their assigned out-of-class work, either by making oral presentations, or by turning in written work. It is important that the students realize that "we don't do disposable work."

Presentation is the phase where the new material is introduced by the teacher in the form of an expository lecture or a narrative, or demonstration, or by reading from a text. Often the teacher uses various visuals germane to the area of study. Video or multimedia can be very effective presentation tools. Presentation can at times be made by students. This phase is extremely important as is sets the model from which the students will learn.

Classroom activities make up the phase when students perform various assignments, individual or collaborative, among which are: problem solving, case studies, discussions, exercises, role playing, games, experimenting and demonstrating. These activities may be of at least two levels of complexity: basic (guided activities) and advanced (independent practice).

The difference between these levels is as follows: basic activities are to be accomplished according to patterns or simple models, with little flexibility in their implementation and controlled by the teacher. This is done on purpose because the objective here is to develop initial skills, imitating a certain sample and using particular limited knowledge.

Advanced activities are less controlled (some teacher guidance and support can be helpful, nonetheless), and allow for more freedom and flexibility in their implementation. Students are not limited in their performance except by the task, setting and purpose of the particular activity. Examples of practice are dramatization and project presentations. An important aspect of all activities is the application of the new material and skills in real-life situations or simulated practice, whether it is in the classroom, on the computer, in homework or in field and community activities outside school.

Homework is vital for providing further, independent learning, real-life applications and experiences; it is also needed for assuring retention. Home assignments extend classroom learning and as such should include creative, rather than just regurgitating tasks, (e.g., collecting information or samples, interviewing or helping people, searching for and processing information for a project, solving a problem or writing an essay).

After the homework has been corrected, and if need be, revised to be brought up to standard, it is posted in the classroom. A classroom full of high quality student work provides a model for more high quality output. When the class bulletin boards are full, old work is taken down and put in a portfolio for the rest of the term. This honors the work, and provides a quantitative and qualitative record for teachers, students, parents and administrators.

Closure is the phase in which you review the lesson and offer the summary of the lesson's key points. It might be useful to invite students to review the main points of what they have learned and ask them questions on the lesson. It also includes a general appraisal (assessment and evaluation) of the students' work and a short preview of the lesson to come. Closure is important as it leaves a lasting imprint in students' minds as people usually remember what was said in the beginning and in the end of the conversation.

Last but not least. Instructional support includes everything needed for successful teaching and learning during a lesson, for example, teaching and learning materials, visuals (charts, pictures, text on the posters), manipulatives and realia. Also critical to the contemporary classroom is technology in terms of the hardware and software, which allows for more efficient knowledge presentation and effective learning, and presents the teacher the option to make an otherwise traditional synchronous environment asynchronous. The lesson as a procedure takes place in an actual physical environment comprised of a classroom set up to enhance the learning process (e.g. the specific placement of desks and chairs for optimal perception of information and effective activities, visuals and instructional materials hung on the walls, fresh air and sufficient light).

Suitable **accommodation** can help ensure the learning process for every student. Some accommodations for EL students are:

- Allowing extra time when necessary for a student to complete the task. Understanding the students' developmental level, their abilities, learning styles (e.g. tactile, kinesthetic, visual, auditory), weaknesses and strengths, challenges they face, and making appropriate modifications.
- Providing vocabulary work as well as bilingual dictionaries and handout glossaries.
- Offering to clarify definitions of words and concepts using culturally based analogies.
- Engaging in appropriate level English grammar and vocabulary to make the curriculum more comprehensible to ELs without compromising the quality of what is taught.
- Integrating peer teaching and collaborative activities including all students.
- Using bilingual teacher aids when available.
- Having individual consultations after class when necessary.

After you have completed your teaching and students their learning, how will you know if they have learned and achieved the planned learning outcomes? You have to assess and evaluate their performance to know if the lesson was successful. In the next chapter we will focus on assessment and evaluation which will tell you if you work was done effectively.

CHAPTER 7

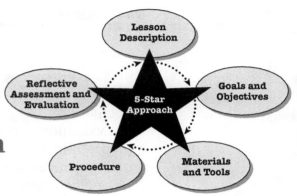

Assessment, Evaluation and Reflection

First Iteration

The teacher's first responsibility is to assist students in their learning. *Ongoing assessment is the teacher's primary instrument in identifying the best way to help the student. Measuring how much a student has learned, in turn, gives us valuable information about the efficacy of the lesson plan and the instruction. Within the appraisal process an enlightened teacher needs to know the difference between assessment and evaluation, what the characteristics of each measurement tool are, and when best to use them to enhance the learning environment.*

Learning, to be successful, must be assessed and evaluated so the student and the teacher know the current state of the student's knowledge, skills and development. These two terms are commonly confused, while there is a significant difference between them.

> **Assessment** is an appraisal of the learner which is inherently reflective. It is based on teacher's observing a student's performance and guiding him or her towards the learning objective. It is dynamic and continuous, and does not imply judgment.
>
> **Evaluation**, on the other hand, is judgmental by nature; it is static and represented by a grade, a rank, or a score that is a snapshot of how well a student does on a particular test on a particular day.

Assessment is directed at the future, giving the student an opportunity to improve, whereas evaluation is a finite event, after which the student may not have a chance to do a better job.

Assessment has two sides: it may be performed by the teacher, and it can be done by the students himself/herself; then is becomes reflective.

Evaluation is done by the teacher or professional evaluator using a prepared instrument, such as test, quiz, exam, or written essay. It is critical to understand grades should be earned by the students; they are not given by the teacher.

Reflection is a careful consideration of one's own actions; it may become a process of self-analysis that may help identify one's strengths and weaknesses. Reflection is a useful instrument for one's development and growth.

Assessment: _____

Evaluation: _____

Reflection: _____

In the 2nd and 3rd iterations of this chapter we will discuss all aspects of assessment, evaluation and reflection in detail.

Second Iteration

* *

This iteration will focus on describing two major teacher's instruments that appraise student's performance and identify his or her weak spots, which will help the student do a better job.

Assessment:_____

_____

Evaluation: _____

_____

Reflection: _____

_____

Coming to Terms Over Assessment, Evaluation and Reflection

. . . .

Perhaps one of the most frequently used terms in modern pedagogy is the word assessment. Within educational circles assessment has come to imply a panoply of meanings including: grades, scores, rubrics, criteria, evaluation, performance, proficiency, plus both formative and summative judgments. In fact, the wide area of multiple meanings encompassed by the word assessment has made it, in terms of common usage within the field of education, more and more often interchangeable with the term evaluation. Is there a difference? The short and unfortunate answer is no. Assessment and evaluation have come to be used synonymously in the area of educational discourse. However, the longer answer is that there should be a difference, and there is an etymological root for such a clear distinction.

The authors believe the lack of discernable difference between assessment and evaluation in the professional vernacular is most regrettable. It may well be that the lack of distinction between these two words has lead to so-called "assessment" tools (e.g. SAT, MSAT, GRE, etc.) which traditionally have acted as evaluations and have had a well documented history of determining the academic futures of millions of students, based on a norm referenced ranking system. That these so-called assessment tests are dispositive of whom is admitted to higher levels of learning in a sense contradicts the original meaning of the idea of assessment.

In fact, **assessment,** which is inherently reflective, is derived from the Latin *assessio*, which literally means, "to sit beside." If one can imagine an examiner sitting alongside a student and providing feedback (based on observing, documenting and analyzing the learner's work), we can better understand how the student is to accomplish genuine assessment, which is ultimately self-assessment. The assessor provides information, however, it is the assessed who must accept or reject the findings.

● WHAT'S THE PLAN?

How are you going to assess your students? (**Hint:** *How would you conduct on-going informal discussions with students to identify their strengths and weaknesses?*)

_____

_____

_____

_____

_____

Too often the information from an evaluation (e.g. a standardized test) is seen as conclusive proof, used to separate the wheat from the chaff (e.g. for purposes of acceptance to a school), and students simply believe the results of a so-called assessment tool that are actually evaluation tools. Assessment requires the critical step of reflective self-assessment. Such a misuse of the concept of assessment (that should aid a learner to know his or her strengths and weaknesses) has provided a basis for schools improperly and unethically to use so-called assessments as an exclusionary tool. Giving precise definitions of words commonly used in a pedagogic discussion brings greater clarity in professional discourse and better serves the purpose of assessment and evaluation as distinct areas of judgment.

The authors argue that the concepts of grades, scores and rankings be stricken from the definition of assessment. Therefore the emphasis on assessment should be the empowering act of the learner to experience self-review based on the feedback by a qualified examiner. Ultimately, requisite learner reflection brings about new self-knowledge.

Evaluation is a static event that is represented by a grade, a rank, or a score that is a snapshot of how well a student does on a particular test on a particular day. On the other hand, an **assessment** is a dynamic process that serves as a point of departure to better know oneself. Therefore, assessment is a procedural phenomenon while evaluation is a finite occurrence.

● WHAT'S THE PLAN?

When and how is it appropriate to evaluate you students? *(**Hint:** When is formal testing (e.g. true and false, multiple choice, or essay exam) most appropriate and what form might it take?)*

_____

_____

_____

_____

_____

In order to avoid this all too common ambiguity, specific attributes to better describe these two terms are presented below (Fig 7.1).

Assessment and evaluation form a relationship, which is both complimentary and vital to the educational process. Concepts of both instructional time and educational paradigm are quite distinct. Let us first consider how time plays a critical role in the difference between assessment and evaluation. An assessment is fundamentally an evolutionary process of enhancing one's self-knowledge based on the feedback that continuously helps the learner to adapt to different learning environments. Assessment is not restricted by time. It is like the continuously changing image of the movie.

On the other hand, an *evaluation* is like a freeze frame of the movie. It is always limited to a certain time period. Recall evaluation is a one-time glimpse of a student's knowledge expressed in a score, ranking, or grade that exists at a given point in time. Accordingly, the difference between assessment and evaluation is similar to the difference

● **FIGURE 7.1**   **Comparing Assessment and Evaluation**

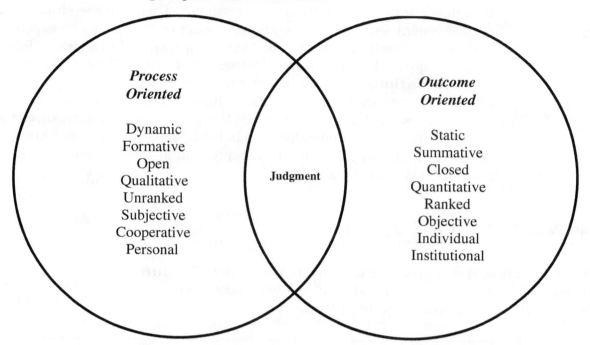

Process Oriented

Dynamic
Formative
Open
Qualitative
Unranked
Subjective
Cooperative
Personal

Judgment

Outcome Oriented

Static
Summative
Closed
Quantitative
Ranked
Objective
Individual
Institutional

Assessment   Evaluation

between animation and still life. These two forms of pedagogical judgment reside in different paradigms—one centered on the learner, the other more concerned with the program or a school. In an assessment one is compared only to himself or herself to better know oneself. In an evaluation one is compared to others primarily to better understand the efficacy of a program or an entire institution.

Reflection is the process of introspection in which you analyze your past actions, behaviors and motives. Reflection helps you understand them and make the necessary improvements for future.

John Dewey (Dewey 1938) once remarked that learning is not merely acquiring information, but making that learning relevant to our everyday life. So, reflection is a tool for continuous improvement of your teaching. The ability to reflect critically on one's experience, integrate knowledge gained from experience with knowledge possessed, and take action on insights is considered by some adult educators to be a distinguishing feature of the adult learner (Brookfield 1998; Ecclestone 1996; Mezirow 1991). Needless to say, reflection is one of the main tools of the teacher's professional development.

Grading

> *Teachers do not give grades; students earn their grades.*

Grading is a judgment of a student's work based on measurement and numerical evaluation. It may become confusing for both students and teachers if different ranking systems are used. The best policy might be a traditional 100 point scale. All assignments are given a certain number of points according to their educational value. The total of all assignments in a term should be equal to 100 which makes it not only easier for you to calculate the final grade but also easier for a student to conceptualize. A score is a point total which is part of a tangible grading criteria. The score is then applied to an accepted scale which yields a letter grade, for instance:

> *Scoring Scale*
> *100–93 = A*
> *92–85 = B*
> *84–75 = C*
> *74–60 = D*
> *59–0 = F*

While it is easy to sum up the points for an objective test (e.g. multiple choice or true and false), it is more difficult to score a short answer or an essay test. Fair and accurate evaluation in reflective writing demands that both the teacher and student be aware of published tangible grading criteria.

The element of quality is at its root subjective. The element of quantity, on the other hand, is an objective measure. To eliminate either of these two elements from grading would lead to an inferior conceptual model. Moreover, a universal philosophical Law of Transformation of Quantity into Quality states that quality emanates from quantity (Engels 1975). This law can be illustrated via skill development where the only way for a skill to develop is through sufficient practice.

For grading criteria to function successfully, it must be viewed as dispositive by both the evaluator and the person whose work is being evaluated. Therefore, a judicious mix of both the factors of quality and quantity in a written assignment are outlined in a five-point scale which asks the student to demonstrate higher order critical thinking skills (i.e. analysis, synthesis and evaluation) by means of a written composition:

1. Complexity of ideas (cogent response to specific question)
2. Quality and quantity of detail (e.g. relevance to the topic, clarity of understanding the issue and expressing your opinion, depth of knowledge of the subject, exactness and fullness of responses, application of the new knowledge, and explicit connections to course materials and used sources)
3. Organization (standard format, e.g., APA)
4. Linguistic Correctness (grammar, syntax)
5. Fluency (determined by amount written)

Grading, unfortunately, can cause anxiety for both the teachers and the student. Let's look at three aspects of grading:

- Grading on the bell curve
- Giving grades versus earning grades
- Helpful hints for grading policies

The bell curve is commonly thought of as a "balanced" curve. This notion is based on the idea that a bell-shaped curve in some way "proves" the validity of a test. In short, a test that results in a few A's and F's, a larger number of D's and B's and a great majority of C's appears desirable to many. The thought is that because the scale resembles the "perfect" bell curve of such a test must be "fair".

The problem is these beliefs are unwarranted and even more importantly may do great harm to students. In fact, a perfect normal distribution curve does not inherently have anything to do with fairness—the bell curve is but a theoretical concept.

For an example of how the bell curve mentality operates against setting and then achieving lofty goals, look at the real world. If you were a surgeon who, year after year lost as many patients on the operating table as you saved would you consider your record "perfect" and expect to open a successful private practice? If you were a home builder who turned out as many good homes as defective ones–with many average homes in between, how long do you think this "perfect" distribution would keep you in business?

When you find that a certain segment of the class does not understand the lesson you can either accept the failure as part of a "bell curve," or intervene to re-teach and retest. If you wish to give a "fair" chance to all, start by using different approaches to appeal to different learning styles, using more effective strategies and activities, contacting parents to enlist their support when students appear to be falling behind, and adjusting your lesson plan.

Your professional responsibility is to produce lesson plans that contain evaluation systems that actively work to bring all students up to standard. Be a committed student advocate. Your success is not premised on the pseudoscientific "perfect" balance of failure and success, but on the number of students who have learned.

As a teacher, are you expected to give grades? If you think the answer is "yes"—think again. Grades should be earned by the students, and not given by the teacher. Think of it this way. Students are the players who score the points, and teachers, in assigning grades, are merely the score keepers. As a teacher you cannot give what you don't have. Grades, after all, are the product of student achievement. Therefore grades are not something "supplied" by the teacher.

Here are some helpful hints to assigning fair grades:

- Grading policy must be fair, straightforward, simple, clear, objective, and understood by the students and their parents.
- A concise handout outlining the grading policy should be distributed by the teacher at the beginning of each term or made available on an Internet site.
- Students should have immediate access to their current grades at any given point during the term.
- You should give periodic updates to the parents. This can be accomplished by an Internet site or by phoning parents with progress reports.

Your grading procedures should be "an open book." While you manage the procedure, it is the student who controls his or her academic future by earning good grades.

> ### *Students are accountable for their own grades.*

At the end of a given evaluation, points are summed up to reveal the scores to be translated into the grades each student earns. Accountability is a learned behavior Students should learn to be accountable for their own grades. A student in your classroom needs to understand by way of your personal guidance and grading policy that the responsibility for his or her grade

Evaluation Tools and Techniques

We commonly use the following evaluation tools in the classroom:

- Test
- Exam
- Quiz
- Essay

Test is an evaluation instrument intended to measure the student's knowledge or skill according to preset criteria. There are various tests, e.g. alternative response, matching and the most popular—multiple choice and standardized tests.

Exam is another evaluation instrument commonly used to measure the student's knowledge and skills by the completion of a particular course of study.

Quiz is a brief evaluation instrument used in education to measure growth in knowledge and skills.

Essay is a written composition on a certain topic.

Which tests are best? A short answer might be that the widest variety of testing provides the learner with multiple ways to demonstrate to the teacher what he or she has learned. So, when many types of tests are given, both teachers and learners have various forms of evidence of learner accomplishments.

Using many different kinds of evaluation tools may be the best way to get the most "snapshots" of what a student knows. Nevertheless, let's remember that learning involves critical thinking skills. Recalling that reflective thought is synonymous to higher order thinking, an essay exam is clearly more apropos than an objective true and false or multiple choice test.

An essay is a much more demanding examination of critical thinking skills. In a successful essay a student must:

- Introduce an organized coherent answer
- Move from information to meaning
- Discuss logical connections
- Sum up the critical points
- Come to conclusions

A student's writing is one of the most valid tests because a student must integrate various language and higher order skills to be successful. An effective answer to this kind of test can reflect a depth of knowledge not present in an objective exam (e.g. true and false or multiple choice tests).

Reflection

Reflection is a process or the result of a process of a person's retrospective analysis of his or her actions. It is one of the most effective instruments of personal and professional growth. Teachers use reflection for their professional development. Students should be taught reflection to develop their self-assessment skills, metacognition and improve their higher-order thinking skills.

Your Turn—Practice Sheets

Please write out five different assessment and evaluation techniques for the class you are teaching or plan to teach. Connect them with the planned learning outcomes. Reflect on the options and alternatives you have for both assessment and evaluation.

Planned Learning Outcomes: _____

_____

_____

Assessment: _____

_____

_____

Evaluation: _____

_____

_____

Reflection: _____

_____

_____

Third Iteration

• •

In this iteration we will further consider the concepts of assessment, evaluation and reflection as effective tools of teachers' and students' growth.

Learning to Assess, Revise and Reflect

An important part of learning is a developed ability to self-assess and learn, and to be able to critically analyze oneself and one's work. We have to help our students to learn to review, reflect and improve. Revision, which is a reflective process, is also an integrative procedure that requires refinement of thought. When a student reshapes assigned tasks he or she actually discovers new and hopefully more meaningful ways of perceiving knowledge.

To revise, a student must have acquired a level of communicative skills, understood some information, and conceptualized an alternative course of action. Clearly, revision can enhance reflective thinking and should be viewed by all as a normal and valued way to enhance one's ability to clarify one's ideas.

Revision is clearly a learner-centered process. As a teacher you should set an environment where this activity is not seen as punishment or reprimand but as an opportunity where the student can choose to be empowered by reengineering better work.

For example, let's consider revising an essay. Clearly, it is the student who must, in the final analysis, reevaluate his or her writing by reflecting on what was written (i.e. embedded knowledge), why it was written (the rationale behind the work) and how it can be modified (e.g. word choice, grammar, logical connections and conclusions). For a reflective writer it is not enough to impart information; what is called for is meaning.

● WHAT'S THE PLAN?

How would you present the concept of revision to your students?
(**Hint:** *How can you make revision part of a learning process rather than a perceived chore?*)

_____

_____

_____

_____

_____

Student-teacher-parent conference

> *Parents Know More Than Children.*

An assessment process that includes a student-teacher-parent conference, where the student acts as the presenter, is a wonderful way for the learner to assume greater control over his or her education.

This three-way process, or troika assessment model, allows the student to become an active participant in an on-going process of assessment. The teacher's role is that of expert assessor, while the parents' contribution is one of expert personal knowledge about their son or daughter. In should also be noted that parental involvement in this process brings huge value to the conference and facilitates follow-up measures (Fig. 7.2).

Both assessment and evaluation require documentation. Documentation which might serve as a basis for these conferences are archived quizzes, tests, homework, essays, audio or video files—in other words, the student's typical work that may be found in his or her portfolio. While sharing the contents of one's portfolio, it is the student as the presenter who explains the *what, how* and *why* of each artifact (Fig. 7.3).

The central idea is to connect in a three-way mutual problem-solving process that highlights student accountability where the student articulates how he or she, via the evidence supplied, is building small successes into larger ones.

● **FIGURE 7.2**   **Student-Teacher-Parent Conference**

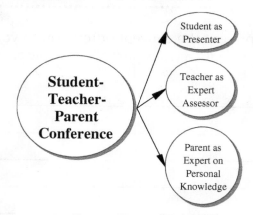

● **FIGURE 7.3**   **Portfolio**

Although there is a clear focus on the student's cognitive development, the affective component of greater self-esteem and personal satisfaction are of immense significance. Students who achieve, and can explain how they achieved, grow in a sense of self-efficacy and are more likely to continue to be successful in future endeavors. Students who do not achieve deserve to get help in developing a clear understanding of their shortcomings and failures.

The goals of conferences are to:

- Educate the student-presenter to the process of self-assessment
- Promote acceptance of responsibility on the part of the student-presenter for academic development and social growth
- Enhance the student-presenter's higher order critical thinking skills to analyze, synthesize and evaluate on an on-going basis

- Pursue open and honest communication among all parties and if need be, revision of student work

This procedure can be carried out in a traditional classroom, over the phone, or even asynchronously over the Internet. What is important is that it is an on-going process designed to give the student an opportunity to present his or her work and receive valuable feedback.

● WHAT'S THE PLAN?

How would you go about setting up a Student-Parent-Teacher Conference? (**Hint:** *Would you use portfolios? How often would you hold the conferences? Would all conferences have to be held at school? What would you as a teacher recommend to address specific student weaknesses?*)

_____

_____

_____

_____

_____

Authentic Assessment and Evaluation, and Metacognition

Authentic assessment and evaluation occur when a teacher makes a direct examination of the learner's performance on a given task. Authentic assessment and evaluation are more than just the learner's recall of information—it requires the student to perform a task that will be judged. For instance, there is a difference between writing about hitting a ninety mile-an-hour fastball thrown by Roger Clemens and actually doing so! Performance is the key ingredient in authentic assessment and evaluation.

In the classroom, instead of students marking a T or F, or selecting one of four options on a multiple choice quiz, or making decisions on a traditional test, an authentic appraisal can be seen in a portfolio where a wide range of students' works, such as writings, video clips of activities and performances, records of assignments and discussions and other artifacts is to be accumulated over the course of study.

Authentic tests have more inherent validity in that they examine responses in a real world environment. For example, let's consider a piano recital. The pianist must focus his or her comprehensive knowledge on one musical piece with skill and artistic creativity to be successful. A pencil and paper test on how to play Bach is at best simplistic and at worst seems a bit silly. The needs of learners appear best supported by authentic testing that applies to the real world in which they must live after the three o'clock school bell rings. As for the teacher, it seems clear that it is easier to assess a student and also improve teaching methods based on an authentic assessment rather than try to interpret the proxy items of a traditional test, which are indirect indications at best of a skill or of comprehensive knowledge.

There is a link between authentic assessment and evaluation, and metacognition. When we think about how we think we also are assessing how well we do. This process is called metacognition.

Metacognition can be defined as "cognition about cognition," or "knowing about knowing." It helps identify how a student learns and how he or she uses strategies to learn or solve problems. Metacognition develops via self-analysis and reflection. As a learner becomes successful in a number of learning situations, there occurs a recognition that certain learning strategies are better than others and some can transfer from one situation to another. For example, the knowledge of a strategy in acquiring basic vocabulary appears to be the same whether one is studying history, math, science, or even a foreign language. Not only are certain learning strategies transferable, but many skills including language skills can be transferred. For instance, there never was a good writer who was not first a good reader. Correspondingly, math skills are critical for developing problem-solving skills in sciences like physics and chemistry. In a holistic sense skills are interdependent.

It is a critical notion when building an effective lesson. This point has very important implications regarding the curricular base of lesson plans for a population ever more culturally and linguistically diverse. When we look at bilingual education, for instance, we need to note that language acquisition is a skill-based enterprise. Therefore, in learning to read English it is essential that the learner of English as a foreign or second language know how to read in his or her native language. One cannot transfer a skill one does not possess.

Awareness of how one thinks is a valuable learning tool. Teachers have a role to play in modeling metacognitive behaviors. To model metacognitive behavior one must be focused on process as well as outcomes.

In short, metacognition is critical to the ultimate goal of education—the emergence of a lifelong self-directed learner—a learner who knows how he or she learns. Such a learner knows not only how he or she learns but is better able to articulate what and why they learn.

● WHAT'S THE PLAN?

How do you decide which kind of test (authentic, true and false, multiple choice) best fits the needs of your lesson plan? (**Hint:** *What kind of knowledge and to what depth are you asking students to demonstrate?*)

_____

_____

_____

_____

_____

_____

Now that we have looked at the appraisal of student performance and can both assess and evaluate learning, let's reflect and refocus—based on your observation, teacher-student conferences and measurements—on how best to continue to construct knowledge and skill development in the classroom.

CHAPTER 8

Knowledge Construction and Skill Development

First Iteration

When you plan your lessons, you should understand how students learn. People do not just acquire new knowledge; they construct it in continuous interaction with the existing knowledge, the environment and each other, engaging in analyzing, problem solving, generating new ideas and living their experiences. This process is called knowledge construction. Along with building new knowledge, students develop certain skills that are necessary to meet life's various challenges. It is the teacher's major task to create an effective learning environment that contributes to this process.

People learn by gradually constructing knowledge from pieces of information available to them. In a formal educational setting knowledge construction can be more effective when it is based on certain goals and objectives that connect to their previous knowledge. The process of knowledge construction is conducive for the student's growth when the information is meaningful to him or her, when it is placed in the real-life context, and students can interact with it using their own understanding, goals, and intrinsic motivation. Knowledge construction is enhanced when it takes place in a social environment where students can collaborate, cooperate and communicate integrating all the new information in their life.

Skills develop in a different way, through continuous practice in applying new knowledge in realistic situations. For instance, in order to learn the new word, the student has to use it in various communicative situations, listening, speaking, reading, and writing it many times. Any skill gets better with practice.

When writing your lesson plan, you have to clearly understand what information you will present. In addition, you have to conceptualize different methodologies to reach every student. This is because different students process, use and retain information in different ways. Therefore you must prepare a wide variety of activities to meet the learning needs of each of your students.

Knowledge construction is: _____

_____

Skills develop through: _____

_____

In the 2nd and 3rd iterations we will discuss various aspects of knowledge construction and skill development.

Second Iteration

· ·

This iteration will delve into the heart of learning: how do students learn? How do they construct new knowledge and develop effective skills?

Knowledge construction is _____

_____

Skills develop through _____

_____

Coming to Terms Over Knowledge Construction and Skill Development

· ·

Knowledge construction and skill development is a gradual process involving many factors, such as learning goal, language, environment, situation, social interactions, communication, and instructional methodology, as well as individual student characteristics, including attention, motivation, preferred learning style, etc.

Knowledge—the sum of what is known; the body of information acquired by humankind; in education—the information, concepts, principles and facts students have to master according to state standards and learning objectives. Knowledge is not acquired; it is constructed.

Knowledge Construction—a dynamic, active process in which learners constantly endeavor to make the meaning of new information.

Skill—the learned capacity to carry out pre-determined results in an effective way. Among them are basic skills (reading, writing, listening, speaking), communication, critical thinking, problem-solving and learning skills. Skills are developed.

Skill Development—skills are developed through structured, continuous procedure or training in continuous interactions and applications whereby people learn how to perform a certain operation in the most effective way.

Learning Process

How do children learn? They gather information and experience the world around them. They pick up the pieces that are meaningful and essential to them, experiment with them, and put this new information and experience together. Such learning exemplifies constructivism, a concept that emphasizes the importance of the knowledge, beliefs, and skills an individual develops through engaging with the reality and integrates into learning. It recognizes the construction of new understanding as a combination of prior learning with new experiences. Raw data found on the internet, primary sources selected in the books, and interactive materials and tools provide the basis for inquiry and experiences that students can use to build new knowledge. This process can be stimulated by the teacher's open-ended questions, prompts and modeling, and by students' own interaction, reflection and experimentation with the new knowledge, as well as collaboration and cooperation in the classroom.

The teacher who understands how the knowledge is constructed creates an environment, outlines the learning outcomes, sets up problems and facilitates students' inquiry and exploration, giving them the necessary support and promoting new patterns of thinking. The teacher listens to students as they discuss ideas and experiment, and gradually shifts the balance of responsibility to the learner. Learning can take unexpected turns as students are given independence to manage their own explorations which should not upset the teacher.

In this course of action, the teacher should encourage students' higher level thinking. The process of knowledge construction challenges students to reach beyond the simple and limited factual response. It encourages students to connect and summarize concepts by analyzing, synthesizing, predicting, justifying, probing, arguing and defending their ideas.

If the classroom can provide a stress-free environment where students can freely exchange their personal views and test them against their peers' ideas, each student will continue to build knowledge based on empirical evidence. Hands-on activities, collaboration and observations of the real world provide new shared experiences for this construction.

John Dewey believed education depended on action. Knowledge and ideas emerge only from a situation in which learners draw them out of experiences that have meaning and importance to them. These situations occur in a social context, such as a classroom, where students join in collaborative work thereby creating a community of learners who build their knowledge together. Jean Piaget considered children to be active and motivated learners who, through numerous interactions with their physical and social environments, construct an increasingly complex understanding of the world around them. To reach an understanding of basic phenomena children have to autonomously discover relationships and ideas in classroom situations that involve activities of interest to them. Understanding is built up step by step through active involvement.

Lev Vygotsky's theory suggested that social activities are often precursors to, and form the basis of complex mental processes: children initially use new skills in the course of interacting with adults or peers and slowly internalize these skills for their own, independent use.

● WHAT'S THE PLAN?

When preparing a lesson plan, consider how your students will be constructing new knowledge. What strategies and tools for it will be most effective? (**Hint:** *Think of engaging students both in independent exploration and in problem solving as well as in communication and collaboration with the peers.*)

_____

_____

_____

_____

_____

Your Turn—Practice Sheets

Please explain what strategies and activities you will include in your lesson plan for constructing new knowledge and developing new skills.

Introduction _____

_____

_____

Presentation of the New Material _____

_____

_____

Student Basic Activities _____

_____

_____

Student Advanced Activities _____

_____

_____

Assessment and Evaluation _____

_____

_____

Closure _____

_____

_____

Third Iteration

* *

This iteration is about teaching and learning: what do teachers have to do to make students learn?

What Does it Mean, to Learn?

What do we really know about how we learn and the role of the teacher in the learning process? We acquire knowledge when we are involved with meaningful content. This means that if we are merely imitating or simply repeating something, we are not genuinely involved in the learning process. The key notion is active engagement where you construct your own unique understanding by using your prior knowledge (things you already know and believe) combined with the new knowledge that you experience each day. That means we are constantly involved in asking questions and solving problems on our own or with others. Understanding how we learn and how we can grow each day in our knowledge gives us a strong indication of which teachers can truly help us in the learning process. An instructor that demands memorization, recitation and repetition might be a good indoctrinator—but hardly an effective teacher.

The indoctrinator presents his or her "true knowledge" and then expects the student to deposit this knowledge in his or her brain as one might deposit money in a bank. Later the student can "withdraw" this "deposit" on a quiz or test. This kind of learning is not well integrated with prior knowledge. The student merely sets up a memory transmission capacity based on someone else's notion of truth.

Of course, this does not mean that all memorization is bad. On the contrary, memorizing multiplication tables, a Shakespearean sonnet or your favorite prayer can have great merit. The point is memorization as a singular teaching technique is more suited for a particular task. On the other hand, an effective teacher actively engages his or her students in "give and take" inquiry sessions and acts as guide and a co-explorer who promotes the notion that each student should form his or her own conclusions.

This idea of learning via point and counter point is as old as Socrates. Enlightened teachers ask you to question, challenge and then make up your own mind with a deeper understanding of what you believe and why you believe it. This more insightful comprehension is a function of what we call higher order critical thinking skills. Think of critical thinking as a three-step process consisting of:

- Analysis (new knowledge),
- Synthesis (new knowledge + prior knowledge) and
- Evaluation (what you think is of value to believe and retain).

The road to learning winds down many pathways—pathways that we construct in our quest for truth.

Yes, we are different as individuals because we think and conceptualize in distinct ways. The first thing to be emphasized is that human beings construct their own meanings. This knowledge becomes the way people understand the world in which they live. Realizing how knowledge is constructed, we can harmonize teaching and parenting practices to help youngsters learn. If we accept the notion that each person comes to build their own conceptions and conclusions about what is real, we open up the possibility of unique ideas and solution sets. The results can lead to enlightened thought. A case in point, for centuries many people generally believed that the sun rotated around the earth. Others however, constructed their own meanings about the movement of planets.

In the 17th century Galileo constructed his very controversial "new knowledge" (yes, there were earlier constructs on a heliocentric system from the Greeks, Arabs and Indians along with math calculations of Copernicus) that proved the earth rotates around the sun.

A constructivist approach allows for an individual search for truth. So how can we encourage the "Galileos" of today? Let's look at seven steps you can begin to implement right now:

- Ask open-ended questions to spark a free exchange of ideas.
- Use words in your questions that incorporate action verbs: predict, list, identify, state, describe, define, solve, compare and contrast, classify, and create when framing a question.

- Permit instructional conversations to be student-centered and student-driven. This may require the teacher or parent to modify strategies and content.
- Nurture dialogue by seeking continuous elaboration of a youngster's first responses.
- Practice patience by allowing sufficient wait time after posing questions so students construct connections among ideas.
- Use analogies.
- Point to ideas or experiences that possibly contradict a youngster's first hypotheses and continue a thoughtful discussion.

As you are having this instructional dialogue remember questions should be meaningful for the student or at least be of rising importance. We all can become self-motivated when questions involve our prior knowledge and then move beyond to incorporate new information. It is in realizing the connection between old information (prior knowledge) and new information (what is to be learned) where we build new connections as we ponder revised and refined insights. By seeking the student's viewpoint we are giving it inherent value.

Recall the need for patient listening, questioning, agreeing or challenging that is related to the student's suppositions – not a necessarily preconceived agenda. Students learn best when we appreciate their agendas and conversely when they are aware of and value certain curricular goals.

Don't forget that real learning takes place in the real world and that social contexts have much to do with how we perceive what is true; these social contexts can be a springboard to a deeper and more meaningful exploration of the truth.

Learn-Centered Education

What is education for? Is it for the teachers to teach, or for the learners to learn? Let's discuss a learner-centered classroom. We know that students' beliefs about their abilities have a lot to do with their motivation to construct knowledge. While it is a common belief that motivation precedes action—actually some cognitive psychologists believe just the reverse. The argument is that when a student takes on a task he or she would rather not do, that learner can be influenced by other students who are doing that same task successfully.

Not wanting to be left out, our student attempts the task and then realizes that a task is doable. At that point motivation seemingly emerges. Thus, we end up with a developmental sequence of action, motivation, and happily more action!

Of course, in this example what is key is that others in the classroom provided a model for our student, which yielded a positive response to a learning task. A learning-centered classroom occurs within a social context where the class, as a group, can construct knowledge.

Certain identifiable groups of students (African American, Latino and Native American) have had traditionally less success in school than other groups. The reasons for low achievement have much to do with grinding poverty and the soft bigotry of low expectations. For such traditionally unsuccessful students—and any other struggling students, a learner-centered classroom where everyone is involved can create the enriched learning environment they deserve. Moreover, leaner-centered classrooms that employ a culturally responsive curriculum to excite the students' social conscience can also help provide a quality educational experience.

Old assumptions about the "winners and losers" in a school based on race, ethnicity or poverty can be rendered irrelevant when schools gear their instruction to use students' prior knowledge and adapt to a wide variety of learning styles. We know that success builds on success. So, once a student's initial experiences in the school result in achievement, that student enjoys an elevated sense of self-efficacy (the, "Yes, I can!" attitude).

To organize a learning-centered classroom teachers need to set up an academic environment where students can collaborate, cooperate, problem solve as a group and establish a peer teaching and learning atmosphere. Research strongly indicates that in these kinds of learner-centered classrooms, not only do students find the learning more meaningful—they learn more than in the traditional classroom setting.

To sum up, high expectations, nourishing environment, peer teaching and other group activities that present a student the opportunity to see how other students solve problems are methods that can produce a world-class education. So much of learning is not about the what, but about the how, that is where "students teaching students" under the guidance of an enlightened teacher can have a tremendous impact. Learning together is a hallmark of a learner-centered class, and one in which academic development is accelerated while social skills are clearly developed.

A few questions for you to ponder on:

- How do people learn?
- How do you visualize the process of knowledge construction?
- What are the essential conditions for effective knowledge construction?
- What, do you believe, is the role of the teaching in the process of knowledge construction?
- What does the process of skill development look like?

The lesson plan, while being the main focus of this workbook does not function in isolation. Instead it is a vital part of the learning process that emanates from prior lesson plans or prior student knowledge and leads to yet another lesson. The lesson plan is a link in a chain of learning that connects one idea to another. Now let's consider how we are going to achieve intended learning outcomes via strategic and tactical planning. Chapter 9 will consider the organizing, structuring and modeling that takes place within your lesson plans. These notions are not to be thought of as static ideas but as dynamic concepts that allow for multiple approaches in planning and implementing a lesson to meet the needs of your students.

CHAPTER 9

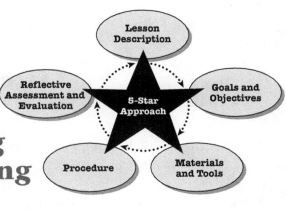

Organizing, Structuring and Modeling in Teaching and Learning

First Iteration

A lesson plan is a product, and a lesson is a process. As a product, a lesson plan provides a model of the future lesson for developing a knowledge base and concomitant skills. As a process, a lesson is intended to organize the teaching and learning events, and make it effective by thoughtful structuring. So when you plan a lesson you actually attempt to organize and structure the learning process to achieve the best learning outcomes. The resulting plan ensures a systematic way to achieve success in the classroom (e.g. learning to read and then reading to learn). Social Learning Theory is based on the premise of human observation and imitation. The model of the lesson you, as a teacher, create can elevate or lower the quality of learning that occurs.

You probably realize that education is organized learning. Organizing learning requires planning, and the latter is the foundation of education. Creating a lesson plan involves planning for learning experiences. Lesson planning helps to structure instruction, learning, classroom practice, and your time. This eventually makes your teaching performance more efficient, less stressful and, what is crucial, rewarding for you. Most importantly, a well-constructed lesson plan sets a pathway to productive learning for your students.

Thorough lesson plan development is a precondition for effective teaching. The 5-Star Lesson Plan is designed to make your teaching performance smoother and at the same time less time-consuming.

Organizing: _____

Planning: _____

Modeling: _____

In the 2nd and 3rd iterations we will discuss all aspects of organizing, structuring and modeling in detail.

Second Iteration

• •

This iteration will examine the concepts of organization, structure and modeling in teaching and learning.

All educational programs are designed according to plans, and these planning strategies emanate from your curriculum. The lesson will be a success when it is carefully organized and structured. Organization provides the teacher with the guidelines which will help ensure effective lesson implementation and lead to the preset learning outcomes.

Does planning affect a teachers' professional behavior? It certainly does, as research and experience show: planning helps teachers remain focused on the topic they are teaching and effectively manage limited lesson time based on the selected structure, affecting the way teachers organize students' learning and interact with them.

To organize the lesson means _____

_____

To structure the lesson means _____

_____

A model of the lesson is _____

_____

Coming to Terms Over Organizing, Structuring and Modeling

• •

Organizing means arranging separate elements into one whole, e.g. various learning activities, assignments and resources into a coherent lesson plan where everything is interconnected and works for common goal, or 30 individual students into a class functioning as one team.

Structuring is organizing elements in a certain way, in a pattern or a construction for better performance.

Modeling, or simulation, is another side of organization and structuring. It means designing in a certain way, imitating some form, or making a pattern.

When you prepare a lesson, you actually create a lesson prototype, an organizational structure of an instructional process you are going to implement in your class. If you look at the lesson plan you have just developed from this perspective, you will realize that it is actually a model of your future lesson (Serdyukov 2002). It will define not only *the what, how, and when* of your lesson but also organize all of it based on a selected structure and time to hold all classroom activities together.

How do you structure and organize a lesson? We know that a lesson consists of several interconnected components: instruction, new material presentation, student activities, assessment and evaluation, and closure. This is a generic structure of the lesson. The lesson develops according to this structure. Each of the components, in turn, has to be structured and organized. For instance, in the introduction you may start by greeting the class and asking students how they are doing today. Then you announce the topic of the lesson, explain what students will be doing and what outcomes they will be expected to achieve. You can write the lesson plan and outcomes on the whiteboard. You should also bridge the new topic to the students' previous knowledge and background. This may be a way to organize your lesson introduction.

Presentation of the new material also should be organized according to a certain structure you choose. For example, you can start by asking you students a few questions on the topic. If they will study electricity, you can ask them how it is generated, and how they use it. Then you can show them pictures of electrical stations, generators, solar batteries, electric circuits and appliances. After that you can start explaining what electricity is, and how it works. Maybe you will interrupt your presentation with questions to keep students engaged. The structure of presentation depends on the material you teach, students' preparedness for the topic, the best way you know students will perceive and process information, the instructional tools you use, and lesson's goals and objectives.

Now you understand you organize the lesson and each of its components according to the structure you select. For each lesson you identify the structure based on its goal, objectives, learning outcomes, students' level of knowledge and abilities, instructional content, your methodological views, and available instructional materials and tools. For each component you determine its specific objective, materials, assignments, activities, and tools.

The most important component of any lesson is student activities—it is there they communicate, collaborate and build their knowledge and develop skills. Try to organize students' learning in such as way that they are continuously engaged in learning, are on task and do their job right.

● **W H A T ' S   T H E   P L A N ?**

Identify the structure of student activities component in your lesson. (**Hint:** *Think of selecting and organizing all activities in such a way that students gradually build their knowledge and develop their skills. See that these activities aim at achieving the desired learning outcomes.*)

_____

_____

_____

_____

_____

While we discussed possible organization and structure of the introduction and new material presentation above, and you organized student learning activities, closure plays an important part in student appreciation of the lesson and in retaining the new knowledge. Recall what closure is about.

● **W H A T ' S   T H E   P L A N ?**

Design the structure of the closure. (**Hint:** *Think of student performance, of their achievements, of what they have accomplished, and of what they will learn at the next lesson.*)

_____

_____

_____

_____

_____

Modeling/simulation is a technique we often use in education. For example, when you teach your students to cooperate and collaborate while solving learning tasks, you create collaborative situations in which they work together. This will not only help them construct new knowledge but also model real-life, collaborative, problem-solving situations that they will encounter more than once in their future jobs.

When you present a new topic, material, or problem, you try whenever possible to construct or imitate a practical example. Thus, if you teach math or physics, you demonstrate how problem-solving can be applied to real-life tasks through using a model of an actual situation. When you teach English as a Second Language (ESL) or some foreign language, you help your students to master patterns of the target language use: typical colloquialisms and expressions, standard phrases, and sample dialogues.

Last but not least, everything you do in class verbally or nonverbally, emotionally or cognitively sets a model. In other words, what you, the teacher, do and how you behave, communicate, interact, inherently set a model that students will for better or worse, consciously or unconsciously, imitate. Therefore, a professional educator always is attentive to everything in him or her: the attire, professional conduct, communication, passion and care for students.

Many of us have fond memories of a favorite teacher. In choosing a teaching career we now realize what a profound impact he or she may have had on our lives. That is the power of modeling. We remember that former teacher not only as a competent instructor but also as a caring human being. Education to a great extent is modeling. Organizing, planning, structuring, and modeling are some of the "secrets" of a quality education.

● WHAT'S THE PLAN?

According to research, 80 percent of teaching is modeling. What are the traits, both personal and professional, you as a teacher wish to model in your class?

_____

_____

_____

_____

_____

Your Turn—Practice Sheets

Now construct a model of the lesson based on the principles described above.

1. _____

_____

_____

2. _____

_____

_____

3. _____

_____

_____

4. _____

_____

_____

5. _____

_____

Third Iteration

* *

This iteration will expand on the issues of organizing, structuring and modeling in teaching and learning.

All educational programs are designed according to plans, and these planning strategies emanate from your curriculum. A successful plan provides for a highly reliable learning process, and ensures students' achieving their learning outcomes.

Does planning affect a teachers' professional behavior? It certainly does, as research and experience show: planning helps teachers remain focused on the topic they are teaching and effectively manage limited lesson time, affecting the way teachers organize the learning and interact with their students.

When you prepare a lesson, you actually create a lesson prototype, an organizational structure of an instructional process you are going to implement in your class. If you look at the lesson plan you have just developed from this perspective, you will realize that it is actually a model of your future lesson (Serdyukov 2002). It will define not only *the what, how, and when* of your lesson but also organize all of it based on a selected structure and time to hold all classroom activities together.

When you give your students assignments in the classroom, see that these assignments are meaningfully related to the students' background and potential application in real life. For instance, if you want your students talk about food, you can set an atmosphere where students express genuine interest in doing a particular assignment by suggesting they are hungry and you are going to take them to a (virtual) restaurant. Show them a video clip about a restaurant, or a couple of slides showing restaurant views, give them several menus from the restaurants, and suggest that they order food according to their liking. If you role play, breaking the class into pairs where one student will play the role of a customer, and the other will be a waiter, will create a fun activity with very effective outcomes.

● WHAT'S THE PLAN?

As you think about lesson plan strategies and activities, what, in your opinion, is the difference between transmitting information and engaging students in a meaning-centered activity? (**Hint:** *think of the distinction between mere information and meaning—which do you think better engages the student?*)

_____

_____

_____

_____

_____

Modeling/simulation is a technique we often use in education. For example, when you teach your students to cooperate and collaborate while solving learning tasks, you create collaborative situations in which they work together. This will not only help them construct new knowledge but also model real-life, collaborative, problem-solving situations that they will encounter more than once in their future jobs.

When you present a new topic, material, or problem, you try whenever possible to construct or imitate a practical example. Thus, if you teach math or physics, you demonstrate how problem-solving can be applied to real-life tasks through using a model of an actual situation. When you teach English as a Second Language (ESL) or some foreign language, you help your students to master patterns of the target language use: typical colloquialisms and expressions, standard phrases, and sample dialogues.

● WHAT'S THE PLAN?

As you think about lesson plan strategies and activities, ponder the relationship between the lesson and the students' own prior knowledge. Write down an activity that you believe will "connect" with your students. (**Hint:** *In order to make your curriculum culturally* *responsive you need to model a real life situation that relates to the background that the students bring to the class.)*

_____

_____

_____

_____

_____

Last but not least, everything you do in class verbally or nonverbally, emotionally or cognitively sets a model. In other words, what you, the teacher, do and how you behave, communicate, interact, inherently set a model that students will for better or worse, consciously or unconsciously, imitate. Therefore, a professional educator always is attentive to everything in him or her: the attire, professional conduct, communication, passion and care for students.

Many of us have fond memories of a favorite teacher. In choosing a teaching career we now realize what a profound impact he or she may have had on our lives. That is the power of modeling. We remember that former teacher not only as a competent instructor but also as a caring human being. Education to a great extent is modeling. Organizing, planning, structuring, and modeling are some of the "secrets" of a quality education.

Other Approaches to Lesson Planning

There have been quite a few attempts to design an effective lesson plan structure. One of the most well-known is Madeline Hunter's 7–step lesson plan (Hunter 1982) which in some aspects is different from our 5-Star Lesson Plan. Hunter's steps were as follows:

1. Objectives
2. Standards
3. Anticipatory set
4. Presentation
5. Guided practice
6. Independent practice
7. Closure

This 7-step lesson plan is useful, however it does not specifically mention an important component of a lesson—the reflective assessment and evaluation of students' performance and outcomes. Homework assignments and homework checkup and are two other important phases of the lesson that should also be included in an effective plan. Finally, an introduction is needed in the beginning of the lesson to initiate the lesson for students and prepare them for learning.

The lesson plan, while the main focus of this workbook, does not function in isolation. Instead it is a vital part of the learning process that emanates from prior lesson plans or prior student knowledge and leads to yet another lesson. The lesson plan is a link in a chain of learning that connects one idea to another. Now let's consider how we are going to achieve intended learning outcomes via strategic and tactical planning.

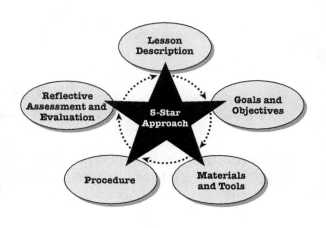

CHAPTER 10

Course and Lesson: Strategic and Tactical Planning

First Iteration

Understanding short and long range planning and how your lesson plan fits into a sequence of lessons to present new knowledge and skills while reinforcing previous learning is part of a well-planned learning process that can become your modus operandi for delivering the most enriched curricula to all students while using the widest variety of methodological approaches.

While working on a lesson plan, it is important to remember that a lesson is not a stand-alone piece in the course: it is just one section of the process, and it is usually devoted to a particular topic; it naturally stems from the previous lesson and, at the same time, lays down the foundation for the subsequent lesson. That is why, when designing a lesson plan, we have to take into account the lesson's position in the course system. As a part of a sequence it provides connections to both the previous and subsequent lesson in the course.

Therefore, we can talk of two kinds of planning: **strategic planning**, a long range design of a particular course (e.g. math may be taught differently than English literature). On the other hand, **tactical planning** is a short range design focusing on the different aspects planning a lesson (e.g. the 5-Star Lesson Plan) or a unit extending for a few days.

Strategic Planning: _____

Tactical Planning: _____

In the 2nd and 3rd iterations we will address the peculiarities of both types of the planning.

Second Iteration

• •

In this iteration we will define the two types of planning, strategic and tactical, and identify the place a lesson occupies in the course.

Coming to Terms Over a Lesson in the Course

Besides discussing a lesson plan, let us take a look at the position a lesson occupies in a course. A **course** delivering a certain subject matter or specific content represents a particular area that can be considered as a whole. The **lessons in a course** are its constituent parts, each of them being derived from another and dependent on the others. In the instructional process they extend sequentially through a certain period of time (a year, a semester, a quarter, a month, a week or a day) and together form a complete single whole, both as a system and as a continuum.

A course can be broken into some blocks commonly united by a topic. These blocks are called units. A unit consists of several lessons. So, a course as a system has a hierarchical structure:

● **FIGURE 10.1   Course Structure**

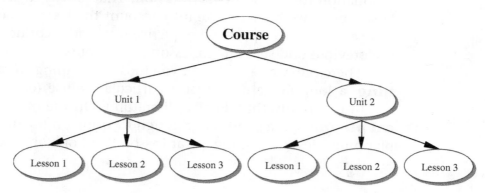

● **FIGURE 10.2   Course Sequence**

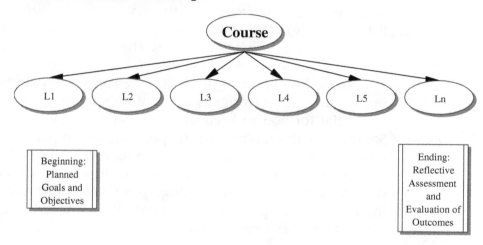

As a process, a course is a sequence of lessons that unwrap one-by-one along a timeline. This is a continuous process that begins when the course goals and objectives are stated, and ends when the learners' outcomes are assessed and evaluated and reflected upon. Thus, each course can also be described as a linear sequence of lessons.

A single lesson consequently can be presented as a sequence of various activities, both teacher's and students', organized around the lesson goal, objectives and outcomes by a plan.

● **WHAT'S THE PLAN?**

Give an example of a lesson plan that links to the previous lesson and creates a bridge to a future lesson.

_____

_____

_____

_____

_____

_____

Therefore, we can talk of two kinds of planning: a long-range design of a particular course (e.g. math may be taught differently than English literature), and a short-range design focusing on the different aspects of planning a lesson (e.g. the 5-Star Lesson Plan), or a unit extending for a few days (a week).

These two kinds of planning, **strategic** and **tactical,** have different rules. Here we focus on tactical planning. However, it will be beneficial for you to keep in mind the strategic aspects of planning. So, try to maintain links to the previous lesson, when you start a new one, by reviewing it or referring to its main points. In addition, try also to make projections for the next lesson, when concluding the present lesson. It helps to bridge past and future learning providing integrity and wholeness of the content area or subject, and facilitate acquisition of the new material.

Your Turn—Practice Sheets

Please select a lesson in the course you teach and describe the position it occupies there. Explain the connections between this lesson, its preceding and subsequent lessons.

Lesson Topic and its Connections _____

_____

_____

Goal, Objectives and Outcomes and their Connections _____

_____

_____

Activities and their Connections _____

_____

_____

Assessment and its Connection _____

_____

_____

Third Iteration

In this iteration we will demonstrate an algorithm of the lesson plan which will explain how learning takes place.

An Algorithm of a Lesson Plan

A lesson plan can be presented in the form of an algorithm (linear, branching or iterative) using the "If . . . then . . . ." logical formula. An **algorithm** is a predetermined set of operations leading to an intended outcome. A medical prescription or a cooking recipe are, in essence, algorithms. An example of the iterative algorithm for a homework checkup activity is presented below.

● **FIGURE 10.3**

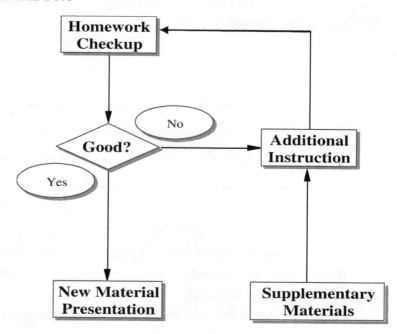

The algorithmic procedure is implemented as follows: A homework checkup is an operation in which a teacher checks a student's preparedness for the lesson using various instructional tools such as questions, tests, quizzes, oral reports, and written papers. If the student's homework is found good (yes), the teacher can move on to new material presentation.

If the work does not meet preset criteria (no), then additional instruction is provided that can be supported by supplementary materials and other activities. Thus, the cycle continues until the student passes the checkup satisfactorily.

Actually, this loop represents a classic learning cycle (see Chapter 6). The procedure is a standard pattern of an instructional process that reflects typical classroom practices.

● WHAT'S THE PLAN?

Considering the algorithmic procedure, how can you set a successful learning environment? (**Hint:** *Consider re-teaching. Recall your job is to help raise students to meet standards.)*

_____

_____

_____

_____

_____

_____

Learning cycles form an inherent pattern. Patterns are a major element in lesson plan implementation. Any pattern in your lesson plan will not suffice; the step-by-step design of the lesson plan and as will we see its implementation, must be well-coordinated and congruent. All learning cycles are intertwined in the spiral of continuous learning.

CHAPTER 11

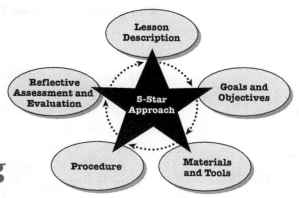

Time Efficiency in Teaching and Learning

First Iteration

*W*e have just seen how reflective assessment and evaluation are about appreciating, measuring and judging learning. These functions are an inherent part of education. One thing you will constantly measure in the classroom is time. Research on the concept of time demonstrates its critical value as an integral variable in any lesson plan. Effective use of the lesson time through time management is a sure way to achieve effective learning outcomes. This chapter will outline the best uses of time from the traditional classroom periods punctuated by school bells to online education where an asynchronous design treats time in a much different manner.

Time is a most significant commodity for a teacher and for a learner because it is always scarce and thus demands modifications in curricular and methodological considerations. These changes affect your lesson plan. Making teaching and learning more efficient via the clock is a challenge: it calls for better instructional strategies, tools and management.

Although in a general sense it is always better to have more allotted time to increase the prospects of engaged time, in reality time is always limited for all participants of the learning process, therefore within the lesson itself timing and pacing of activities is crucial. Student achievement depends in great measure on the efficient use of every moment in the classroom.

An accurate allocation of time for activities during lesson planning is critical for the lesson plan successful implementation. On a broader scale, to cope with the challenges of education in the 21st century, instructors have to come up with new, effective strategies of facilitating, guiding and assisting students, while the students have to be taught to develop effective time management and independent learning skills. This will help both learners and teachers to be successful in dealing with educational tasks and problems within certain time constraints to enhance learning productivity. It will help them to be better prepared for life and work requirements.

Making the learning process more effective by minimizing waste of the learning time, we may expect more learning to take place in less time which will result in achieving the planned outcomes with greater efficiency. The formula of effective learning thus is:

The more time sensitive, organized and effective the instructional system, the more opportunities for the student to be engaged in the learning process, and the greater the effort and concomitant achievement.

It is worthwhile to make students understand they are ultimately responsible for their learning. The classroom education can provide an instructor-facilitated learning environment, but a student, in order to sustain success, must each day become more and more a self-directed learner accountable for his or her learning outcomes.

Time in teaching and learning is: _____

_____

In the 2nd and 3rd iterations we will discuss various aspects of time management.

Second Iteration

This iteration explains how time affects teaching and learning, and how a teacher should learn to manage his or her time.

Time in the Lesson Plan Is _____

_____

Coming to Terms Over Time

Time is the lesson plan is like the mortar that keeps all components and procedures together.

"Time can be considered an absolute factor that affects a given learning experience. The allocation of time is the single most controllable, and therefore, one of the most powerful operational decisions a school can make (Ryan, 1991)." According to Oakes (1985), time emerges as a pivotal element in the effectiveness of an institution.

Bloom (1980) wrote that time on task is one of the variables that accounts for learning differences between students, between classes, and even between nations (Fig 11.1).

● **FIGURE 11.1**

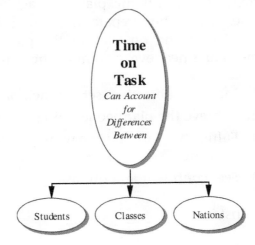

Although in a general sense it is always better to have more allotted time to increase the prospects of engaged time, in reality time is always limited for all participants of the learning process, therefore within the lesson itself timing and pacing of activities is crucial. Student achievement depends in great measure on the efficient use of every moment in the classroom. ***The secret of effective learning is thus to increase time on task (to keep students engaged in learning activities) in each lesson while reducing non-learning time to a minimum (Serdyukov and Serdyukova 2006). Therefore, optimal time planning of all lesson activities may contribute to a more efficient use of the limited lesson time frame and produce improved learning outcomes.***

Time, as has been shown, is a crucial factor in education: any program, course or lesson is limited in time. Time is a critical teaching constraint limiting all your intentions and implementations. It is also one of the major factors of success of an organized activity. Recall, a lesson plan is *a model of organized learning events within a standard time period of a formal instructional process*. Without organizing learning by structuring it and assigning time values to planned activities and without sticking to them whenever possible, there will be little chance of attaining your goals and reaching the outcomes.

A high school lesson, for example, is usually 50 minutes long. You are in charge of facilitating that your students achieve the planned outcomes. This is why a lesson plan and its components must be assigned weighted time for their implementation so that the teacher can fulfill the plan and achieve the desired goals and outcomes. In lesson preparation you normally calculate the time you intend to spend on each of the planned activities. You write these time values near every point of the plan so that you can:

1. Meet the objectives set for each of the procedures,
2. Achieve the planned learning outcomes,
3. Fulfill the plan on time without compromising the quality of learning
4. Feel confident and on task

For instance:

- Presenting the new topic: introduction, reading the text, Q&A, discussion, video demonstration—18 min.
- Student activities: small group work (solving problems)—10 min.
- Student independent work—5 min.

- Student presentations—10 min.
- Assessment—5 min.
- Closure—2 min.

● WHAT'S THE PLAN?

When preparing a lesson plan, consider how much time you will allocate to the following procedures. (**Hint:** *Think of the various activities you should select to achieve your planned outcomes.*):

Introduction _____

New Material Presentation _____

Student Activities _____

Independent Practice _____

Assessment and Evaluation _____

Closure _____

Optimal time management contributes to the lesson effectiveness.

One of the purposes of school is to prepare children for real life. Among other things, school helps develop learning skills together with self-management which include time management skills (Serdyukov and Hill, 2005). Students should know how to become effective independent learners which implies they need to learn how to organize and manage their time. Learning to use time efficiently during lessons and when doing homework will make students more effective learners which will serve them well in the real world. One of the teacher's tasks then is to identify and evaluate student time management habits, and develop productive ways to increase time efficiency in the learning process.

Timing Lesson Activities

An accurate allocation of time for activities during lesson planning is critical for the lesson plan successful implementation. You need to calculate how long should each activity take and write the number of minutes for each of the activities. This will allow you to see if you have planned the lesson optimally and can fit everything in. The factors affecting time allocation are as follows:

- Goals and objectives
- The activities you need to implement to have students achieve the planned outcomes
- The volume and complexity of the new material
- Class variables (number of students in the class, student individual abilities and limitations, and their preparedness for the lesson, and time of the day)
- Your experience

If during the lesson you have a plan with time benchmarks to follow, you will feel more confident in achieving the desired outcomes of the lesson. Certainly, you cannot follow your plan precisely minute to minute because there may be various circumstances, such as more time spent on student questions during new material presentation, or students requiring more time for solving a problem or completing a project. Nevertheless, if you try to remain on schedule, you have the best opportunity to complete the planned activities.

These variables need to be taken into account in the preparation phase.

- **Class size** impacts the number of activities to be implemented, the structure of group collaborative activities, time allocation for various activities, amount of information to present, and classroom management.
- Knowledge of **student stratification** (e.g. prior knowledge, readiness) for assigning individual tasks and for organizing collaborative work. A helpful solution might be to place students at different developmental levels into heterogeneous small groups. This will ensure better results if peer tutoring and buddy support are used.

- **Students' individual characteristics**: age, culture, language (specifically, ESL proficiency), special needs, attention span, learning styles, interests, habits, manners and personal experiences—all these influence the choice of assignments, tasks and activities, roles to play and communication modes.
- Availability of **instructional tools**, including technological ones, and materials.
- The interval between the current and the previous lesson—in case of an extended period between the classes, a review of the previously learned material may be necessary.
- **Time of day**—people have different perception and attention levels at various times of the day (for instance, the first and the last lessons of the day can be the least productive, while the lessons in the middle of the morning, usually the 3rd and 4th lessons can the most productive).

● WHAT'S THE PLAN?

When preparing a lesson plan, consider your class variables *(**Hint:** Think of how you are going to accommodate the plan according to the following)*:

Class Size: _____

Individual Student Characteristics: _____

_____

_____

Previous Lesson on the Topic Taught . . . . Days Ago, Needs Review

_____

_____

Time of Day the Lesson Will be Taught: _____

_____

_____

Time for Self-Directed Learning

Though schools offer organized group learning, the majority of their work students do independently. Actually, only 8% of their life time students spend in the classrooms; most of the time they learn independently. Let's turn to the challenge of independent planning, time management and self-control. Independent or self-directed learning can be defined as "a process in which individuals take the initiative, with or without the help of others" (Knowles, 1975, p. 11), to diagnose their learning needs, formulate learning goals, identify resources for learning, select and implement learning strategies, and evaluate learning outcomes (Buchler 2003). Self-directed learners are students who take responsibility for their own learning: They take charge and are self-regulated. Students, however, need the teacher to help them realize the importance of effective time management in becoming a self-directed learner (Fig. 11.2).

Learning time efficiency is a critical factor for learners. The theoretical foundation of effective learning is validated as a result of a greater student effort generated in response to improved time expenditures. Such an effort requires effective student time management. Students' self-efficacy is positively related to achievement. It seems clear that a "can do" attitude on the part of the student is necessary in order for education to have its most potent effect. Improving learning time efficiency may lead to better learning outcomes and a considerable

● **FIGURE 11.2**

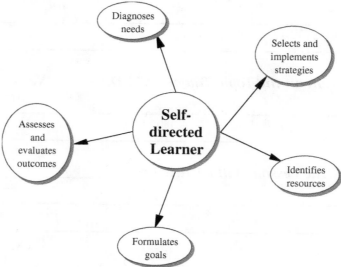

saving of time and energy thus making education more productive. Students should be made aware of how to time their own learning experiences. Perhaps modeling excellent time management in the lessons and mentioning your planning strategies as a teacher will set an environment where students can learn to organize their time. In this way they can set up their own effective study system to be engaged in the learning process and maximize effort over a shorter period of time than is usually required to achieve successful results.

● WHAT'S THE PLAN?

When preparing a lesson plan, consider timing your and student activities:

Introduction _____ *min.*

Presentation of New Material _____ *min.*

Student Basic Activities _____ *min.*

Student Advanced Activities _____ *min*

Assessment and Evaluation _____ *min.*

Closure _____ *min.*

Your Turn—Practice Sheets

Please make a calculation of the planned activities in your lesson plan

I. TIME IN THE LESSON PLAN

Introduction _____ *min.:* _____

_____

Presentation of New Material _____ *min.:* _____

_____

Student Basic Activities _____ *min.:* _____

_____

Student Advanced Activities _____ *min.:* _____

_____

Assessment and Evaluation _____ *min.:* _____

_____

Closure _____ *min.:* _____

_____

Third Iteration

• •

Here we discuss important issues related to time management in education: do we need more or less time for effective learning, how to learn to measure your time, and whether asynchronicity provides more opportunities for learning

More or Less Time?

The issue of learning time efficiency is certainly, not new. There have been studies of time expenditure in school that demonstrated the importance of effective time management for successful learning outcomes. The three trends that seem to follow from these studies are to:

1. Add time to learning,
2. Within the same amount of time continue to upgrade both instruction and learning outcomes, and
3. Try to achieve the same or better learning outcomes in less time (Lozanov 1977; Kitaigorodskaya 1995; Serdyukov 1984; Boyes, Reid, et al. 2004). These three trends may look quite contradictory to each other.

   1. **More time:** There is an understandable tendency in schools, in view of knowledge growth, diversification and specialization, to introduce new content areas (courses) or extend the length of existing courses. Is allocating more time to study an answer to improving knowledge management? There is evidence (Scott and Conrad 1992) that increasing learning time does not produce a significant improvement in learning outcomes. Adding time, according to Metzer (2003), does not enhance learning nor has a profound effect on the quality of learning outcomes, yet it does raise the cost of study. Increasing time for study will be costly for students, schools, employers and taxpayers.

2. **Same time:** Making learning more efficient in the same time frame is certainly reasonable; it calls for better instructional strategies, tools and management. "Time is something we cannot control, but you can certainly rationally and effectively organize the use of it. It is the issue of planning and organizing the process. Using the time effectively now provides the opportunity to use the saved time later. So, continuously saving time develops a stable habit which eventually may lead to raising productivity of learning" (Serdyukov 2005). It should be added that efficient use of the learning time together with optimal planning and organizing, requires a more effective instructional methodology and better teacher preparation.

3. **Less time:** Contracting or compressing the learning time, though illogical at first look, may be a proactive solution. The goal here is to achieve higher learner productivity and make education more time-efficient. Hence a great interest for accelerated and other short term courses. Various approaches and methodologies for providing education in a shorter time without compromising its academic quality have been described in literature (Scott & Conrad 1992; Bowling, Ries & Ivanitskaya 2002, Boyes, Reid et al. 2004, Serdyukov 1984). The most popular is accelerated learning (AL) that is essentially a compressed, short-term course format. One of the fundamental premises underpinning the potential for acceleration or intensity of learning is that the pacing of educational programs must be responsive to the competencies and knowledge of the individual learner (Robinson, 1983). Another premise maintains the idea that people have more intellectual potential for learning than traditional educational formats can make use of (Lozanov 1977). Building upon the principles derived from cognitive psychology, it can be argued that acceleration has the possibility to enhance creativity, outstanding achievement and higher-order thinking skills (Boyes, Reid, et al. 2004). On the other hand, uneconomical ways of managing the learning process and time can reduce actual learning time and interfere with producing the desired learning outcomes. (Serdyukov and Serdyukova 2006).

There is a benefit to each of these options; it depends on the educational institution, format of learning, subject matter, course goals and objectives, student age, and other factors. Whatever option you will pursue depends on you, however the main point remains the same: try to make your teaching and student learning time-efficient by making your lesson more organized and increasing time on task.

Time Logs

To make you planning more effective and understand how students use their time, ask your students to record how much time they spend on particular activities. They can record time by lessons, by days and by weeks. Then you can combine different student logs and calculate average time spent by activity. After that you can organize group work in the class asking students to analyze the data and come up with their evaluation of time usage and ideas for using time more efficiently. This information will also give you the opportunity to rethink your own lesson planning strategies.

● **TABLE 11.1   A Log of Student's Time**

Activities	Day	Week
1. Preparing for the class		
2. Actual time in class		
3. Out-of-class activities		
4. Reading books		
5. Sports		
6. Interacting with peers		
7. Time spent with parents		
8. Communicating with the teacher		
9. Time watching TV		
10. Time spent on the computer (Internet)		

● WHAT'S THE PLAN?

When preparing a lesson plan, think how much time your students need to effectively accomplish a given assignment and activity. (**Hint:** *Think of the time they normally spend on it and try to identify where and how they might save time.*)

_____

_____

_____

_____

_____

Teaching Time

As we know, reflection helps teachers understand what they do effectively in the class and where they fail. Reflection includes analysis of your teaching strategies, your teaching style, relationships and communication with students, and of course, the efficient use of time in the classroom.

● WHAT'S THE PLAN?

As you are developing a lesson plan, think how much time you should allocate to each of the planned activities. (**Hint:** *Think of the time you really need to spend.*)

_____

_____

_____

_____

_____

To better understand how efficiently you spend your time, record the time on various activities for a lesson, a day and a week. Fill in your planned time and then the actual time spent (Table 11.2).

● **TABLE 11.2**   **A Log of Teacher's Time**

Activities	Times Spent (in hours and minutes)		
	Lesson Plan/Actual	Day Plan/Actual	Week Plan/Actual
1. Preparing for teaching			
2. Actual teaching			
3. Field activities			
4. Classroom management			
5. Reading student work			
6. Professional development			
7. Communicating with students outside the classroom			
8. Communicating with parents			
9. Communicating with colleagues			
10. Communicating with administrators and support personnel			
11. Participating in meetings			

When you compare your actual time spent versus the planned time, assess the difference. This will tell you about effective ways of managing the time.

Time in an Asynchronous Environment

When we leave the traditional classroom and consider the late 20th and early 21st century phenomenon of online education, we can see how many of the seemingly immutable facets of time are changed via the concept of asynchronous design where there is no precise timing needed to communicate. Because online education uses computers that access Internet, all communication (email, threaded discussions, wikis, blogs formal essays) can be archived. This allows extra time for the learner to learn at his or her own pace—and for you to read, respond and grade a student without a strict time limit.

In terms of providing time for reflective thought, asynchronous design appears to be inherently superior to the synchronicity of the traditional classroom. Recall the notion of how we learn determines what we learn. The power of the "how" in learning, or what we call the methodology, cannot be underestimated. For example, let's travel back to the 1890's. If you wanted to hear the music of John Philip Sousa and his popular United States Marine Band, you had very limited options. Unless you had a treadle-powered grammophone and had access to Edison and/or Columbia cylinders (the CDs of their time), you had to go to wherever the Sousa band was playing. Even then, you could only listen to what Sousa chose to play. Moreover, unless there was an encore, you could only hear a song once in a performance. Compare that to today where you can download Sousa marches on your computer to your heart's content and listen whenever you want, and as many times as you want.

Now consider the difference between the late 19th and early 21st centuries. It is actually the difference between synchronous and asynchronous design. In short, listening to a specific artist, being at a specific place, waiting for specific time for a single performance or having access to not only Sousa but virtually an unlimited number of musical artists and musical performances wherever you want increases your opportunities to enjoy music. As a student or teacher one can now hook up to the Internet, an iPod or iPad, or other mobile technology accessing curricular information or communicating whenever and with whoever they wish, experiencing imagery and sound as many times as they desire. The opportunities for learning at one's own pace are greater today than ever before. (Fig 11.3).

Viewed as a learning tool, technology that allows for asynchronous design is pedagogically superior to a "live" synchronous performance—and ultimately presents learners (with a multiplicity of learning styles) more ways to understand. Asynchronicity inherently provides more flexibility and opportunities to learn via various modalities.

● **FIGURE 11.3**

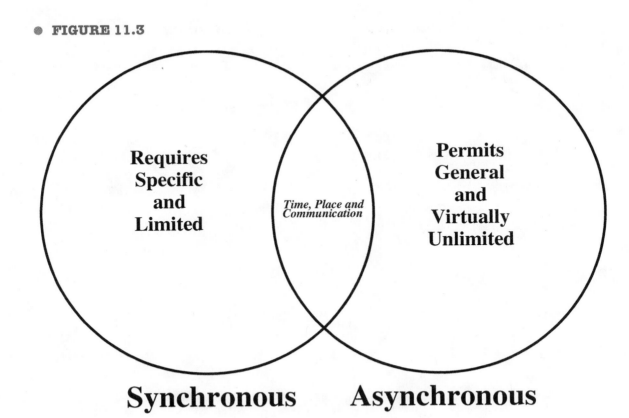

Understanding time as an organizing principle in the classroom is a precondition to an in-depth discussion of knowledge construction and skill development. Organizing, structuring and modeling in the classroom have little value without time. Planning also affects how you teach and how students learn. Consequently an effective lesson plan sets an environment for interactive learning and an enhanced educational outcome.

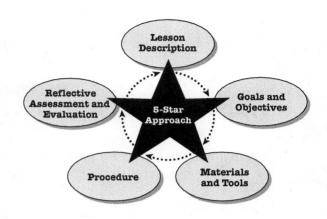

CHAPTER 12

Implementing the Plan

First Iteration

Designing a lesson plan and implementing that plan are tasks that are related yet quite different. Preparing the plan is akin to drawing your own road map to a certain desired destination. Putting that plan into action is like is like driving the car to your predetermined spot. There are many factors that go into implementing a successful lesson plan: the students who attend your class and their individual characteristics, the configuration of your classroom, the access you have to teaching and learning materials, and your skilled implementation of instructional approaches. All these figure into your curricular journey to get you where you want to go.

A lesson is a complex process that has two intermingled sides: preparation/planning and implementation. A lesson plan, thus, is one side of the lesson. The second side is classroom implementation that affects content presentation, students' activities, the use of teaching and learning materials, visuals and technology, and application of instructional strategies, methods and techniques. A good lesson plan, therefore, is not a guarantee of a successful lesson—sound methodological strategies and techniques and a competent and caring teacher are other essential aspects of the lesson implementation.

Lesson Plan: _____

Lesson Implementation: _____

In the 2nd and 3rd iterations we will discuss various aspects affecting lesson plan implementation in the classroom.

Second Iteration

* *

There are many factors that affect the implementation of the lesson plan you designed. You have to be prepared to deal with numerous challenges in the classroom.

Lesson Plan_____

Lesson Implementation_____

Lesson Execution
· ·

Implementation of the lesson plan can be affected by numerous factors, among them student presence/absence, their individual characteristics and behaviors, their preparedness to the lesson, attention level, English language proficiency, your teaching style, your mood and even the time of the day. Thorough preparation and knowing your students together with your teaching and life experiences will help you cope with these problems.

It is helpful to prepare students for the next day's lesson by describing its general outline at the conclusion of the day's lesson, thus setting the anchors, key ideas or anticipatory points for the future class. Likewise, it is beneficial to return to the previous lesson material in an overview or recapitulation of the major points or issues learned in the preceding lesson in the introductory stage. In this way, the teacher builds a continuity of learning, an interrelated sequence of instructional events, a meaningful logical composition of the content pieces in the students' minds which ensures better understanding and retention.

The structure of the lesson may vary according to its goals and objectives. There may be variations in the sequence of the stages, (e.g. activities based on the previously learned material can precede presentation of the new material). Some modules and elements may repeat, (e.g. presentation or cyclic activities can be reiterated several times during one lesson).

Because students certainly have various learning styles, it is important to have several options for the next day's lesson implementation. An experienced teacher always has a backup set of activities, assignments and materials for each lesson in order to prepare for eventualities. There can be additional stages a teacher can introduce in a lesson: a relaxation pause, a physical exercise, a stretching break, a repetition session, a game or a quiz. Any and all can be included in the lesson process if and when the teacher finds it necessary.

● WHAT'S THE PLAN?

*Think how your lesson plan can be affected by various factors (**Hint:** Try to simulate teaching your future lesson in your mind's eye).*

Subject: _____

Topic: _____

*Grade:*_____

*Standards:*_____

Goal: _____

Objectives: _____

Outcomes: _____

Student Activities: _____ *(min.)*

Assessment and Evaluation: _____ *(min.)*

Other Activities: _____ *(min.)*

Affective Component

We are very well aware of the fact that we learn (as well as do anything else) better when we are interested—in short, when positive emotions are involved. Of all of the factors that go into a quality education, the personal and scholastic rapport involving teachers and their students may be the most significant. The core relationship must be built on trust and a mutual desire for students to reach the twin goals of academic growth and social development.

The **affective domain** involves our emotions and values. Inspiration, motivation and empowerment, all affective in nature, express our deepest feelings of self-worth and commitment. One's affective disposition is interwoven into one's cognitive ability.

The teacher's emotional behavior, affective conduct, keen interest and involvement with the students, continuous interaction and communication are crucial for the students' success. The use of humor (your best friend) and the absence of temper (your worst enemy) cannot be underrated. In addition, paralinguistic means of communication: body language, music, visuals, multimedia, play and collaborative activities are the warp and woof of diverse teaching methods to meet the needs of many distinct learning styles. However, when it comes to the affective domain, a teacher's enthusiasm for what is to be taught in the lesson is imperative.

Motivation is a driving force in student learning and is closely connected to the affective domain. Two types of motivation are known: extrinsic and intrinsic, the latter being the more efficient and the more powerful of the two. Let us consider intrinsic motivation as genuine motivation because it resides in the learner. To have a student increase his or her motivation for learning and resulting enhanced achievement, it is vital for the teacher to set an environment where the learner elects to become engaged in goals and objectives. For example, instead of stating the objective as "Students will be able to . . . ", one might say to personalize the lesson: "You will be able to . . . "

Instead of "It is interesting to know", one might posit using analogies to the learner's prior knowledge: "You will be amazed to know that it will help you each day when you . . . ". Besides the personalized goals, role-playing is extremely useful in developing an individual student's involvement in collaboration and in learning. Other factors that are beneficial for setting an environment where the students choose to become engaged through the whole lesson are

- Interesting and relevant content
- Engaging activities
- Enlightened class management
- Continuous teacher's support
- Use of visuals
- Video materials
- Music
- Appreciation embedded in the curriculum of students ever more culturally and linguistically diverse

● WHAT'S THE PLAN?

When preparing a lesson plan, think of the ways to make your lesson stimulating, setting an environment for students to choose to be motivated while having fun. (***Hint:*** *humorous stories, visuals, video clips, multimedia presentations, music, songs):*

_____

_____

_____

_____

Appreciating Students' Individuality and Diversity

One of the most important factors to be taken into account in lesson preparation is individual students' characteristics: their diversity—cultural, ethnic and racial, their special needs, and their psychological individuality—their attention, retention, learning style and behavior. Instructional models appropriate for culturally, linguistically and academically diverse student population should be incorporated into your lesson plans and necessary adaptations developed.

The first precondition to democratic education is equal access. This can be achieved through appropriate planning and using strategies and activities that meet the demands of special needs and Second Language or English Language Learners (ELL). The lessons that serve these learners have five major aims:

- Assist students in their needs
- Help ELL students become proficient in English
- Allow them to participate efficiently in the core curriculum
- Support students' positive self-image
- Promote cross-cultural understanding

Such an approach requires effective English language development that aims at achieving CALP (Cognitive Academic Language Proficiency—J.Cummins), use of students' primary language and cultural background, sheltered academic instruction, scaffolding and students' inclusion in the mainstream academic process.

Research indicates that the academic language utilized in content areas may act as a barrier to the success in school for many ELL students. A critical element in Second Language development is access to comprehensible input in English.

To make content accessible to ELLs, your goal has to be facilitating the gaining of English proficiency while developing in academic areas. The following strategies can be recommended:

- Slow but natural speech
- Clear enunciation
- Short simple sentences
- Controlled vocabulary
- Visual reinforcement
- Frequent comprehension checks

Some additional planning procedures can be recommended for the lesson intended for ELLs:

- Teaching a previously selected vocabulary before presenting new material (presenting new words and illustrating their use in context)
- Preceding written activities by oral activities, such as questions and answers and discussion
- Designing collaborative communicative activities by assigning teams, appropriate roles, and materials
- Using real-life materials and non-educational literature relevant to the topic

An effective contemporary approach to teaching ELLs is SDAIE (Specially Designed Academic Instruction in English), also called sheltered instruction. SDAIE is a synthesis of advanced methodological approaches that have a common purpose of allowing English learners to succeed. Subject matter is delivered in English, whatever the grade level. SDAIE uses language-sensitive strategies, contextual support, and focuses on making instruction in English more comprehensible. Major components of SDAIE are:

- Academically demanding content; authentic, relevant, interesting, and coherent materials and tasks;
- Theme-based and student-centered learning; prior knowledge; contextualized instruction; cooperative learning;
- Positive affective domain;
- Performance-based and authentic assessment.

An integrated language teaching approach provides the necessary foundation for successful ELL learning. This approach focuses on using the target language in context rather than just learning the language. Language is presented and developed in compact and meaningful chunks instead of small unrelated elements. Language experience, both oral and written, should be interwoven with the learning in all curricular areas and in all lessons.

● WHAT'S THE PLAN?

When preparing a lesson plan, consider ELLs' English proficiency.
(**Hint:** *think of how you are going to accommodate the plan according to their level to help them successfully learn the new material*):

*Vocabulary:*_____

Your Speech: _____

Visuals: _____

Comprehension Checks: _____

*Activities:*_____

Other: _____

Lesson plans that incorporate holistic learning, the combination of the social, emotional and intellectual aspects of student development, clearly present a transformational model. Holistic learning can be approached through an appreciation of the theory of Multiple Intelligences (MI). Howard Gardner (1993) posits that students possess a number of different intelligences that can be observed as students solve problems. Intelligence, therefore, is the ability to apply one or more intelligences in ways that a certain community or culture find valuable. MI theory presents a path to comprehend intelligence. Lesson plans that incorporate multiple ways of learning and knowing present activities that reach more students. When students are given choices about how to demonstrate their learning, teachers are transferring some instructional control to students thus making the process learner-centered. The results of that transfer encourage students to build on existing strengths to best comprehend new content and skills.

MI theory works well as a guide to develop lesson plans that meet the needs of a diverse group of learners. The objective is not to teach a specific intelligence (e.g. linguistic, logical/mathematical, visual/spatial, bodily/kinesthetic, musical, naturalistic, interpersonal, intrapersonal) or even to match intelligences with specific activities, but instead to permit learners to use their preferred ways of processing information (i.e. metacognition) and then communicating new learning.

● WHAT'S THE PLAN?

When preparing a lesson plan, consider your students' multiple intelligences. (**Hint:** *think of how you are to going use students' strengths to accommodate the plan*):

Linguistic: _____

Logical-Mathematical: _____

Musical: _____

Bodily-Kinesthetic: _____

*Interpersonal:*_____

Intrapersonal: _____

*Spatial:*_____

Naturalistic (Environmental): _____

The Principle of Balance in a Lesson Plan

> *The end should match the beginning.*
> (Russian Proverb)

An effective lesson plan is a specific systematic educational design aimed at achieving a desired outcome. Like any practical system, in order to function properly it should be balanced. The balance should be among:

- Structure and function
- Structure and content
- Outcomes and objectives
- Your teaching and student learning
- Group and individual work
- Activities and objectives
- The amount of information to be presented and lesson time constraints
- The amount of information to be presented and the amount of information that can possibly be consumed
- Students' level of preparation and content complexity
- Students' individual idiosyncratic characteristics and developmental tasks
- ESL student proficiency and lesson content
- Special Education student proficiency and lesson content
- Learning performance and assessment
- Outcomes and evaluation

The Principle of Balance (Serdyukov 2002) stipulates that all components of the lesson plan must be well coordinated and congruent. When there is an imbalance in a lesson plan or its implementation, the lesson goals and objectives can hardly be achieved (e.g. when the objectives are not supported by adequate activities, or students' outcomes are not matched by valid evaluation)

● WHAT'S THE PLAN?

When preparing a lesson plan, consider all plan elements and assess them in the context of your whole plan. (**Hint:** *try to weigh the elements against the suggested approach and see if your plan is balanced):*

Outcomes and Evaluation _____

Structure and Content _____

Your Teaching and Student Learning _____

Activities and Objectives _____

Group and Individual Work _____

The amount of information to be presented and lesson time constraints

_____

The amount of information to be presented and the amount
of information that can possibly be consumed

_____

Students' level of preparation and content complexity

_____

Students' individual psychological characteristics, assignments and activities

_____

ELL student proficiency and lesson content

_____

Learning performance and assessment

_____

Lesson Assessment and Revision

The plan of the lesson is prepared. What next? Should you start teaching? Before you implement the plan, take some time to review and assess it. The actual assessment will certainly be done by the students who can be the most rigorous critics. You will know of it by observing their work in the classroom, by asking questions and assessing their performance. Still it is worthwhile to give a preliminary educated guess of the lesson and its parts while it is on paper. How? First, the principle of balance can be applied to see if the projected outcomes will meet the objectives. Then criteria for the pre-assessment might be applied. They include the following points:

1. Logical structure of the plan (each subsequent module and activity must stem from the previous one while keeping in mind the overall plan of the course, and be linked to the subsequent module and activity)

2. Activities (Is there a sufficient number of activities to provide for reaching the outcomes? Are they well organized into a consistent system of learning?)

3. Time evaluation for each activity during the lesson (Do I have sufficient time to implement all items of my plan? Do I use the time efficiently?)

4. Accessibility of teaching and learning materials

5. Availability of a contingency plan, in case you run out of time, or vice versa, you have some time left, you have fewer students than you planned for—what would you do?

6. Classroom preparedness

7. Classroom management techniques

You can also use the following checklist to pre-assess your lesson:

- Did I include academic content standards? Are they appropriate for this lesson and for my students?
- Did I clearly state the goal, objectives and learning outcomes?
- Do the subject matter, language material, cognitive demands and activities fit into previous knowledge and experiences as well as students' abilities?
- Will I be able to make the input and learning materials comprehensible?
- How will I take into account students' first languages and cultures?
- Did I integrate all the four language skills into the lesson activities?
- Did I take into account students' multiple intelligences and learning styles?
- Will there be sufficient time for students' individual and collaborative activities, communication, questions and interaction with the materials, as well as relaxation and rest?
- Do I have sufficient visuals, realia and manipulatives?
- Will I make a good use of available technologies?
- Did I include formal and informal assessment and evaluation procedures?
- Will I be able to implement everything I planned in the allocated time frame?

When the lesson has been taught, take time to revise its implementation, reflect and find out where you faltered, or where the plan had been impractical. Make a list of both positive and negative notes, and try to introduce the necessary corrections to the previous version of your plan. Use time logs (see Chapter 11) to analyze your use of time in the lesson. Next time, when you teach the same lesson, you will be fully prepared. Recall: reflection is one of the major instruments of a teacher's professional growth.

● WHAT'S THE PLAN?

Having taught a lesson, review the plan and see what worked and what did not work. Reflect and analyze lesson effective features and flaws:

_____

_____

_____

_____

_____

_____

_____

_____

_____

_____

_____

_____

_____

_____

_____

_____

Your Turn—Practice Sheets

*Please consider various options for the implementation of your lesson plan.
Variability of your planning decisions and different options in the execution
of the plan will help you face the challenges emerging in every lesson.*

IMPLEMENTATION

Subject: _____

Topic: _____

Grade: _____

Standards: _____

Goals: _____

Objectives: _____

Outcomes: _____

Teacher Presentation: _____ *(min.)*

Student Activities: _____ *(min.)*

Assessment and Evaluation: _____ *(min.)*

Other Activities: _____ *(min.)*

Third Iteration

• •

There are things that you cannot miss in your teaching; among them state standards and various other regulations, and your collection of teaching materials you have accumulated for using in the classroom.

State Standards and District Benchmarks
• •

Every state has its own K–12 academic standards, and every district—its benchmarks. In California, for instance, these standards include Curriculum Framework, Content Standards in the subject area, English Language Development Standards, and Teacher Professional Expectations **http://www.ca.gov/cfir/**. When planning a lesson, you should address these standards.

● WHAT'S THE PLAN?
• •

When preparing a lesson plan, consider state standards and district benchmarks (**Hint:** *go online and select those state standards and district benchmarks that apply to your current lesson*):

Subject: _____

Topic: _____

Goal: _____

Objectives: _____

_____

Standards: _____

_____

Benchmarks: _____

Teacher's Lesson Collection

In the course of planning and teaching, every teacher collects a great number of plans and various teaching materials for one's course. It is very convenient to save and maintain the collection of lesson plans and various materials for your subject area or a particular course. A Teacher's Lesson Collection (TELECOL) is a complete set of plans developed for each lesson, together with teaching materials such as texts, visuals, handouts that can be copied as needed, videoclips, computer-based materials, Web-links to parts of the lesson, etc. that the teacher uses in the classroom. This collection is always ready for you to access.

TELECOL may be invaluable when you need a substitute teacher for your class. You can give a complete package for a lesson to your substitute who will then teach along your guidelines using your model and the materials which will guarantee maintenance of your teaching model and quality of work. This collection, certainly, needs to be reviewed, updated and replenished continuously.

Teacher's lesson collection provides the educator with a complete and reliable bank of teaching materials that make teaching easily replicable and as such, more technological and efficient.

A checklist for your lesson collection:

1. Lesson Plans
2. Content (textbook)
3. Additional materials for the content delivery:
   - Books, texts, printouts
   - Visuals (pictures, albums, wall posters, maps, slides, transparencies)
   - Video (tapes, courses, clips, CDs and DVDs)
   - Realia and manipulatives (objects, models, toys)
   - Games (jigsaw puzzles, domino, playing cards, etc.)
   - Multimedia (computer courseware)
   - Web links to relevant sites
4. Technology (computer, iPad, DVD and CD player, Internet hookup, slide projector, overhead projector, TV, tape recorder, video camera, iPhone)
5. Handouts (texts, charts, tables)

6. Activities bank
   - Activities and their descriptions
   - Games
   - Other materials for activities
7. Assessment bank (questionnaires, rubrics)
8. Evaluation bank (quizzes, tests, including computerized ones)
9. Samples of students' work

● WHAT'S THE PLAN?

Make up a list of your own teaching collection:

_____

_____

_____

_____

_____

_____

_____

_____

_____

_____

_____

_____

_____

Now that we have discussed implementing the lesson plan, let's think about the application of your plan not only in the classroom but in the real world where students spend most of their time. One powerful way to best apply your plan is to access your students' families as the human resources you need to extend the school day. Another critical element in your plan is blending standards-based curricula via the social aspects of community life with approaches like service learning. By putting academics in action young citizens not only know their rights but act on their duty to the community.

CHAPTER 13

Extending the Lesson Plan outside the Classroom

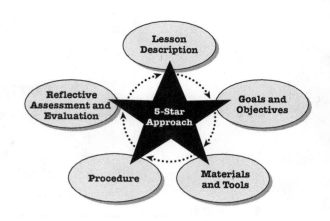

First Iteration

Education is a family as well as a societal affair. In order to best educate a child every resource a teacher can access can prove useful in reinforcing that youngster's educational experience. Because of the limited time that students actually spend in school, your lesson plans need to involve the families of your pupils. Learning also extends from the classroom and school into the community and society on the whole. This chapter will explain the imperative aspect of a learning triangle made up of the student, the parent/family and you, the teacher. The next step and one of the best ways to extend the learning process of your lesson is to engage students in serving their community through service learning and community service.

Do you know how much time K–12 students spend in school? Who are the children's first and most important teachers? Why is it critical for students' success to have parents involved in their learning? How does homework affect students' progress? What is service learning? And how does the community and society affect education?

A family is: _____

Parents are: _____

A community is: _____

In the 2nd and 3rd iterations we will discuss these questions.

Second Iteration

• •

This iteration deals with engaging students with the community and also engaging the family and community with the school.

A family is _____

Parents are _____

A community is _____

Coming to Terms Over Family, Community and Society

A **family** is a group of people affiliated by blood relationship or kinship (father, mother, son, daughter, brother, sister, grandparents). Members of the family usually have common residence, culture and traditions. One of the primary functions of the family is to produce and reproduce persons, biologically and socially. As an agent of socialization, family is the primary source of influence behind the formation of personality and the growth of a child (Wikipedia).

Community is a group of people usually living in the same location and united by some common features, such as nation of origin, culture, and language. They share common values and have a social cohesion (Wikipedia). A family can be a part of the community.

A **society** is a large social grouping sharing the same geographical territory, subject to the same political authority and dominant cultural expectations. Human societies are characterized by patterns of relationships (social relations) between individuals who share a distinctive culture and institutions (Wikipedia).

The First and Most Important Teachers

In the preceding chapters we have outlined the why, what and how of effective lesson plans. We have seen how lesson plans lay out a blueprint for successful teaching and learning. Having said that you can have a well prepared teacher, a well thought out lesson plan and a sincere student who genuinely tries to achieve—and still get failure from that equation.

Why does American education fail so often? Why is it that only 70% of ninth graders graduate with their class? Why is it that about half of all African American and Latino students do not graduate from high school?

To begin to answer this question we must look to the first and most important teachers in the life of a child—the parents. Did you know that a typical student spends only 9 percent of their time in school from kindergarten through 12th grade? In other words, it is a fact that a child from 5 years of age to the young adult of 18 years of age spends 91 percent of his or her time outside the classroom.

We are sure asking a lot from that 9 percent of the time in the classroom! There is an African saying that it takes a community to educate a child. Resources outside the school can make a difference inside the school. There can be no doubt that the exchange of communication between the teacher and the parents as to what is being taught and how parents can play a part in supporting and stimulating their child and in reflective assessment is of critical importance. The traditional one-on-one duo of teacher and student has not proven successful in too many cases. What is called for is a triangular configuration of collaboration between parents, student and teacher.

● **FIGURE 13.1   Time Children Spend in School**

Time Spent in School K-12

☐ 1 Time in School
■ 2 Time outside School

● **FIGURE 13.2**   ● **FIGURE 13.3**

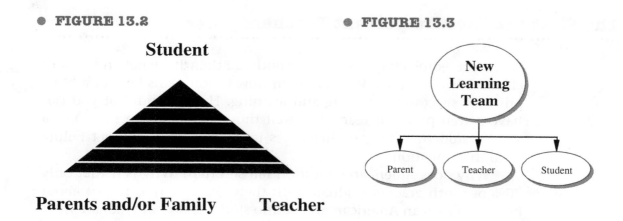

In order to make best use of this limited time frame in school, your lesson plans must involve the parents and/or family (e.g. guardians, grandmothers and grandfathers, brothers and sisters) in the day-to-day learning process. In today's real world of single or even absent parent families and latch-key children, a teacher must find that third party in our triangle. Many times it will be a grandmother or other adult relative, sometimes it will be an older brother or sister. An older brother or sister many times will not only take on the responsibility of looking after their younger sibling, but see right through a younger child's excuses since they do not have to battle through the generation gap! What is important is to find that other person who truly cares about the student.

Involving the parents and/or family in the learning process is the kind of engagement that opens parents' access to monitoring the academic development and social growth of their sons and daughters. It also provides the teacher with important feedback about the child because parents have unique information about the child that the teacher may never know without the parent's assistance. It also gives the opportunity for the teacher and parents to assure a coordinated and straightforward message to the child about the importance and value of education. Research indicates the greater the parent involvement, generally the higher the student achievement. Furthermore, studies on parent involvement reveal that when a child's family is able to develop an environment that promotes learning, sets high expectations for achievement, and takes an active role in school and community, student success may be predicted with a high degree of confidence. This is why teacher-parent communication should be open, frequent and continuous.

Piaget reasoned that children learn best when given the chance to interact with their environments. It then follows that the greater the interaction between children and their parents (e.g. using portfolio of accomplishments and homework assignments) and the community, the greater the likelihood of student success.

An Approach to Homework

We know that successful completion of homework is a major element in improving academic achievement while building stronger family ties. What is called for is not the old hit and miss duo of teacher and student, but a new game plan for a team of three made up of the parent(s), teacher and student.

Let's see how we can recruit and enlist this winning team for every student in your class to keep everyone informed and participating in the educational process.

The teacher's checklist for parent/family involvement:

1. Send a list of month (or longer) of nightly assignments home, to be placed in an easily accessible place for all to see (e.g. on the refrigerator!).
2. Have some assignments involve parents (e.g., their cultural and linguistic backgrounds or professional knowledge and experiences).
3. Make follow-up phone calls or emails to answer parent's questions.
4. Invite parents on a regular basis to see their child work in class.
5. Ask parents to reward effort (as simple and inexpensive as verbal praise) for effort rather than outcome.
6. Send home a portfolio of the student's work on a regular basis so the learner can explain what he or she is doing.
7. Request parents write (in the language of their choice) or express to you in a way convenient to them their assessment of their child's effort.
8. Visit with parents on a regular basis, either at school or in their home.
9. Organize parents' meetings, like a parents' club, once a month in school.

● WHAT'S THE PLAN?

Planning your lesson plans in advance, make a list of 10 homework assignments you can present to your students who in turn will give a copy to their parents. (**Suggestion:** *Let's demystify homework and instead of making it busy work or drudgery think of creative and fun assignments.*)

_____

_____

_____

_____

_____

Let's focus on checklist items 6 and 7. Send home a portfolio of the students typical work (e.g. essays, math problems, science papers, history tests) and ask parents to review it and write to you. Their feedback is powerful because it:

1. Encourages the student to take responsibility for his or her performance.
2. Teaches the value of self-assessment as students reason through their mistakes and problem solve.
3. Improves student's communication skills when he or she explains the what, how and why of his or her work to parents.
4. Opens a dialogue between student and parents on the child's number one vocation in life—that of a student.
5. Makes some use of that 91 percent of the time outside the classroom to extend the learning day.
6. Assists students learn to construct their own meanings as they engage with their parents.
7. Improves student self-esteem as success builds on success.
8. Builds on the ultimate goal of having the student become a lifelong self-directed learner.
9. Allows parents to better understand their children by taking their interests to heart.

● **FIGURE 13.4**

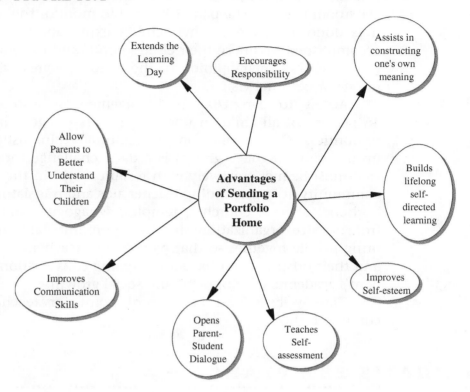

● **WHAT'S THE PLAN?**

Make a list of the kind of typical graded assignments (remember those assignments where students do not meet standards should be in the revision process) that you would put in a student's portfolio. (**Hint:** *Essays and written answers to problems are very valuable in that they demonstrate developing higher order critical thinking skills.*)

_____

_____

_____

_____

_____

_____

_____

It is important to note that the parent does not take the place of the classroom teacher. The parent is there to monitor the work, to be sure it is done, to listen to their child's explanation of what is being accomplished, to praise their child's effort, and to communicate back to the teacher their opinion of the child's progress via letter, email, phone or personal visit.

Access to parent/family involvement is also crucial. Today, 45 percent of all children under five years of age come from ethnic minorities. Communication in a culturally pluralistic society made up of many language groups is a daily challenge for many teachers that must be met creatively with resources within the school and the community at large. Finding teacher aids and translators in the neighborhood, at local churches, temples, synagogues and mosques, and from service organizations in the community are creative ways to bring people together so that parents and teachers as well as parents and their offspring can have an on-going conversation about the student's academic development and social growth.

Class website can be a focal point for teacher-class-parents communication.

● **WHAT'S THE PLAN?**

What are some of the ways you can reach out to your students of different cultural and linguistic backgrounds? (**Hint:** *Culturally responsive curricula, in school bilingual opportunities for every student and community-based organizations all present wonderful possibilities.*)

_____

_____

_____

_____

_____

_____

_____

_____

Your Turn—Practice Sheets

Please design a plan of student community service. Include the activities that will help students connect their classroom learning with life.

Lesson Topic: _____

_____

Goal and Objectives: _____

_____

_____

*Activities:*_____

_____

_____

*Assessment:*_____

_____

_____

Third Iteration

• •

This iteration expands the view on school-community relationships.

Academics in Action
....

Community involvement in the educational process is also critical. Teachers who are able to rally a community to honor education make a real difference in the quality of life as together with the community they weave an economic and social fabric of hope and inclusion. Economically, students secure better jobs via a good education. Socially, the very essence of American society, a participatory democracy via an educated citizenry bodes well a more responsive government. Community involvement can amplify and bring credibility to a teacher's lesson so, in the end young people get a valuable message that can last for a lifetime.

Community involvement can be multidirectional. For instance, community can maintain a high level of student motivation though demonstrating its interest in student learning outcomes. Community leaders, business people and social figures can enlighten the classroom with real-life examples. Students themselves can engage in community life through various channels, e.g., helping elderly people, tidying the streets, planting the trees, taking care of small children, etc. Service learning is both a philosophy and methodological concept that constructs bridges from your lesson plan to the community. This occurs by integrating into your curriculum activities that are mutually rewarding to your students as well as to the community at large. For example, a school poetry festival where the community is invited to hear the student original poems written in their English classes benefits the school, the community, and the young people involved. Likewise school science projects to test the pollutants in the air and water provide a valuable educational tool to everyone in the community. Significantly, research indicates that service learning curricula have led to an increase in student achievement and a decrease in truancy and vandalism.

When teachers are in the forefront of organizing educational events, such as inviting scholars and outstanding figures from community to the school room, education becomes inherently more real and more pertinent. Involving students in service learning—where the school's regular curriculum is blended with a service to the community (a poetry festival for an English class activity, or a food drive to use math skills), students realize that they not only have personal freedom but a public duty to help their communities. Combining academic development with social growth via community involvement begins with a lesson plan that affects students inside the classroom because it is relevant outside the classroom.

Community involvement can take various forms. One of them can take the form of collecting essential information about community life: how the community is structured, what are community centers (services, churches, clubs) and their functions, what are the forms of community activities, how people are organized and participate in the community life. Another direction should be student active engagement in community events: participation in the activities, preparation of public events, helping the sick and poor, cleaning and improving public places.

● WHAT'S THE PLAN?

Think of the ways your students can get involved in community life.
(**Hint:** have students identify various activities and integrate their preparation and/or reporting about them into your lesson plans.)

_____

_____

_____

_____

_____

_____

Now that the family and the community have been incorporated into your lesson plan to best serve the needs of each and every student you teach—it is time to think about you! Chapter 14 will explore how you can improve as a professional educator and how that can be reflected in your lesson plans.

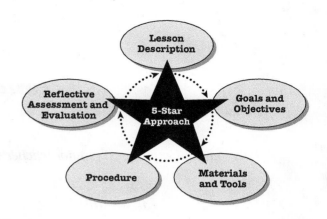

CHAPTER 14

Teacher Professional Competence

First Iteration

A teacher who is competent in the subject matter will still be lacking as a professional educator if he or she he does not follow research-based pedagogical principles and does not possess methodological and social skills necessary to work with the learner in a person-to-person learning environment and help that learner through various social, educational, personal and emotional challenges. Teaching human beings is a multifaceted enterprise. To be an effective educator, a teacher engages in continuous, life-long learning which is a critical part of his or her professional activities. This helps to grow professional competence without which one cannot teach.

The teacher's competence is primarily in two areas: subject matter and pedagogy. These two competences embrace not only sound knowledge in these fields, but also a capacity to help students acquire certain information. In addition, students should be able to apply this information in real life situations. In order to do this, a teacher has to develop various teaching. However, we know all too well that the teacher's work is very complex and multifaceted. So, besides teaching in his or her subject area, a teacher has to be prepared to deal with various social, cultural and personal problems both in and outside class, and be able to effectively communicate with students and their parents.

Teacher's performance fully depends on his or her professional competence.

Teacher professional competence: _____

_____

In 2nd and 3rd iterations we will explain what this competence consists of.

Second Iteration

. . . .

This iteration explains six major teacher's competences.

> **I hear, and I forget. I see, and I remember. I do, and I understand.**
> **(Confucius)**

Coming to Terms Over Professional Competence

. . . .

It goes without saying that quality teaching greatly depends on a teacher's professional competence. Successful lesson plan development is, undeniably, an important part of a teacher's professional capability. What, then, is **professional competence**? It is the ability to professionally perform on the job.

The teacher's work centers around two major areas:

- Subject matter (e.g. mathematics, physics, language, literature),
- Pedagogy (i.e. the art and science, or perhaps the craft of education).

Having noted these two areas, it is important to underline that though you may refer to yourself as an "English teacher" or a "2nd grade teacher", what you really are is a teacher of human beings. In other words, while you must possess a discerning mind in terms of what you teach and how you teach it, you must also demonstrate a compassionate heart based on your passion to serve every child. This is why the concept of student-centered learning is axiomatic in contemporary pedagogy.

● WHAT'S THE PLAN?

What skills and techniques do you bring to teaching? (**Hint:** *Think of your field of expertise and the "people skills" you have developed.*)

_____

_____

_____

_____

However, we know all too well that the teacher's work is very complex and multifaceted. So, besides teaching in his or her subject area, a teacher has to be prepared to deal with various social, cultural and personal problems both in and outside class, and be able to effectively communicate with students and their parents.

One of the greatest disappointments in the life of a student must be when a teacher cannot answer the student's questions about the things that excite that pupil. Last but not least: the teacher's oral and written expression should model a highly literate person—a person who cares about not only *what* they say but *how* they say it.

It is also critical for a teacher to be a well-rounded person, knowing history, geography, literature, understanding music and art—in short, an interesting human being capable of engaging students. In short, as a great Russian playwright Anton Chekhov wrote, "In a human being everything must be beautiful: the face, and the attire, and the soul, and the thoughts". This directly relates to the teacher.

Six Fundamental Competencies

Therefore, we can describe teacher professional competence as a system consisting of six fundamental competences (Serdyukov 2002):

1. Expertise in the subject area
2. Pedagogical competence
3. Socio-cultural competence
4. Communicative competence
5. Technological competence
6. General erudition

● **FIGURE 14.1**

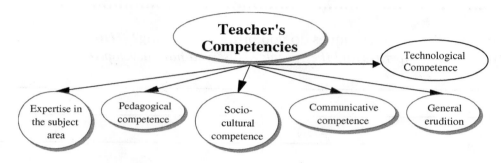

Let us discuss these competences.

1. Expertise in the subject area embraces a particular area of human knowledge, (e.g. mathematics, physics, biology, social sciences, literature, foreign/second language, physical education).

2. Pedagogical competence requires knowledge of basic educational and psychological theories, methods and practices, proficiency or skillfulness in teaching and a caring attitude. Your approach to every student should stem from deeply held notions of fairness, honesty, and professional integrity.

3. Socio-cultural competence results in the ability to teach a diverse student population and be knowledgeable in community-based and service learning. In preparing a lesson plan we should take into account various students' characteristics: their different intelligences and learning styles, their culture, ethnicity, race, previous education, life experiences, attitudes and behaviors. The personal and scholastic rapport between teachers and their students emanating from a culturally responsive curriculum is critical for successful learning. This interaction has been called a "core relationship" of learning. Culturally sensitive approaches can build enduring teacher-learner relationships with students in a classroom ever more culturally and linguistically diverse.

4. Communicative competence allows a teacher to efficiently establish and develop communication with students and their parents, as well as with peers and colleagues. Instruction is essentially implemented through communication between the teacher and students. It should be well-developed because it directly affects students' performance. This student-directed communica-

tion is not narrowed to content delivery only, but includes feedback on their performance, exchange of messages during and beyond the class, and social conversations; in fact, any type of verbal, as well as non-verbal interaction. In short, education is in the conversation!

5. Technological competence helps the teacher effectively operate and apply in teaching various educational technologies. Today's teaching and learning is technology-based—computers, iPads, mobile phones and other gadgets abound, and students use them continuously, outside school and in the classroom. Technology is critical for effective information presentation and retention, for developing various skills, for communicating and collaborating.

6. General erudition includes subjects that are essential for any educated professional, such as knowledge of history, literature and other areas of universal knowledge. Students love and appreciate their teacher's expertise in any subject, cultural background and experience. For example, American history may be your one of your fortes, Russian music, another, football a third.

● WHAT'S THE PLAN?

Which of these six teacher competencies is your strongest?

_____

_____

_____

Which is your weakest?

_____

_____

_____

Professional competence is commonly developed through years of study, teaching practice, life experiences, organized professional development and self-directed life-long learning. Again, overlaying all of these competences is the continual building and nurturing of personal moral standards and principles.

Your Turn—Practice Sheets

Please analyze your proficiency in each of the six major competences and make up a plan for improvements.

*Expertise in the Subject Area*_____

_____

*Pedagogical Competence*_____

_____

*Socio-Cultural Competence*_____

_____

*Communicative Competence*_____

_____

*Technological Competence*_____

_____

*General Erudition*_____

_____

Third Iteration

• •

One of the major components of the teacher's professional competence is methodological competence which directly affects teaching.

Methodological Concerns

• •

We would like to stress here the importance of methodology that, as a part of pedagogy, is focused on practical issues of teaching and learning and on teaching particular subjects, such as ESL, literature, or mathematics. Methodology includes contemporary instructional approaches, strategies, techniques and technologies. It also embraces lesson planning and content delivery together with class organization and management.

Consequently, in methodology courses, lesson plan design and development, class organization and management need to be taught. Learning to write and implement a lesson plan is a very important part of a teacher professional preparation. The teacher is actually a creator and a facilitator of learning goals, environments, activities and outcomes.

Schools of education teach students of education a good deal of theory. What needs to be increased in teacher preparation is the practical experience in all aspects of instruction, akin to what the students of engineering get in real-life problem-solving activities.

Practicing lesson plan design and development is as essential for teachers as experimentation for physicists or chemists, or learning to disassemble and assemble a car engine for an automobile mechanic.

Such an experience can be gained not only through teaching practice (field activities in school) but also through introducing lesson plan development in all methodology courses. This would have a positive effect on the outcome-based preparation of teacher candidates. The lesson plan is an indispensable instrument in teacher preparation. It disciplines teaching.

Activities intended for lesson plan development may include: problem solving, analyzing different plans (found on the Web or presented on paper, in the video format or in a class observation), designing lesson models, developing fragments or full-blown plans and demonstrating them in front of a class.

A very useful activity in teacher preparation is to ask a teacher candidate to videotape a lesson he or she teaches, then review the tape, reflect and write a self-evaluation. The video can be watched in the college class and discussed with the peers and the instructor. Students generally believe it is one of the most efficient professional activities that give them an objective view of their performance.

The lesson plans teacher candidates write should be detailed and precise. Designing extensive lesson plans helps them develop the necessary skills for their future teaching experiences. This training could follow or be part of all methodology classes. When teaching your class, you may not have to design such detailed plans—actually the skills developed in the university classes and in the teaching practice will serve you well even if you write a short plan outlining major instructional and learning events.

Teacher preparation in lesson plan development is, actually, a four-stage procedure:

1. **Analysis**—examination of existing written lesson plans, and of classroom teaching practice observations (live or videotaped)
2. **Synthesis**—new lesson plan design and development
3. **Application**—demonstration of teaching according to the lesson plan
4. **Reflective assessment and evaluation**—appraisal by you, a peer and an instructor

This procedure looks as follows:

● **FIGURE 14.2**

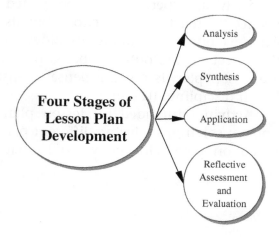

This model of teacher preparation presupposes that the teacher previously acquired adequate theoretical knowledge necessary for plan development, and partially reflects Bloom's Taxonomy of Educational Objectives (1956). It allows a teacher candidate to develop strong lesson planning skills.

Practicing in lesson plan development is an objective in itself: it helps you to master organization, planning and management of the instructional process, develops you as a professional and prepares you for actual teaching.

● WHAT'S THE PLAN?

What lesson plan(s) do you plan on practicing? (**Hint:** *By creating a video clip of your teaching you can see yourself as others see you—assessing your own work as often as you wish whenever you wish!)*

_____

_____

_____

_____

_____

_____

_____

As you work through your professional development, you realize the value of effective planning and organization in teaching.

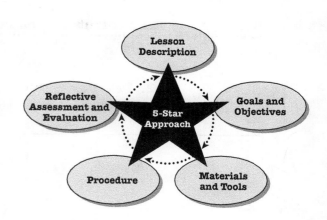

National University Lesson Plan

Lesson Plan Design
···

Subject: _____

*Grade:*_____

Lesson Topic: _____

*Candidate's Name:*_____

ID # _____

Site Supervisor: _____

NU Supervisor: _____

*Date:*_____

1. **Introduction:** (Identify Grade Level K–12, Academic Content Standard(s), rationale, focus learner, create bridges from past learning, behavior expectations)

	Rationale:

2. **Learner Outcome(s)/Objective(s):** (What will students learn from this lesson? How will you measure mastery of the outcome?)

	Rationale:

3. **Pre-assessment Activity:** (Determine students' abilities to achieve the learner outcome and prescribe instruction accordingly. Consider: linguistic background, academic language abilities, content knowledge, cultural and health considerations, interests and aspirations, physical development, social development, emotional development.)

	Rationale:

4. **Differentiation, Adaptation & Accommodation Strategies:** (Based on the pre-assessments, modify Learning Activities based on learner characteristics to meet the needs of ELL & special needs students, highly achieving students and low achieving students)

	Rationale:

5. **Resources:** (Identify materials needed for this lesson accounting for varying degrees of skill level)

	Rationale:

6. **Learning Activities:** Explicit Teacher Instruction—(Explain, model, demonstrate, check for understanding)

Check for Understanding:	*Rationale:*

7. **Learning Activities:** Guided Practice/Collaborative Practice (Check for understanding and provide feedback and re-teaching)

Check for Understanding:	*Rationale:*

8. **Independent Practice:** (Provide practice that supports the learning outcome. Note: Independent activities are assigned assuming that students understand the concept well enough to work on their own.)

Check for Understanding:	*Rationale:*

9. **Assessment and Evaluation:** (Describe how you will assess and/ or evaluate the students' learning. Describe differentiating assessment strategies you will use for ELL, special needs students, highly achieving students and low achieving students.)

	Rationale:

10. **Closure:** (Describe how students will reflect on what they have learned.)

	Rationale:

11. **Lesson Reflection/Assessment:** (Collect student learning data to determine: What went well? What needs to be changed? Were learning outcomes met? What activities will you add, change, modify in the future? What can be done to follow up on the learning from this lesson? Who needs additional help? Who needs enrichment or higher level work?)

Revised: 4/22/10
Note: An electronic copy of the Lesson Plan Design may be found on the Nu-Fast website: **http://www.nu-fast.com.**
Links: Browse Folders–SOE–TED–TED 629–Student Resources Unit 4

National University Lesson Plan Rubric
(For Student Teaching)

Candidate: _____

Date: _____

Supervisor: _____

Course: _____

Lesson Topic: _____

University Supervisors will refer to the Lesson Plan Rubric to give the candidate feedback on their lesson planning knowledge and skills. University Supervisors are not required to complete the rubric and return it to the Credential Department.

(4) Integrating/Innovative—The candidate provides <u>clear, consistent</u>, and <u>convincing evidence</u> demonstrating the competency or competencies. Candidate's practices demonstrate a preponderance of <u>appropriate, relevant,</u> accurate, and <u>clear</u> or <u>detailed evidence</u>. The evidence is <u>purposefully connected</u> and <u>reinforced</u> across this TPE Domain.

(3) Applying—The candidate provides <u>clear evidence</u> demonstrating the competency or competencies. Candidate's practices demonstrate a preponderance of <u>appropriate, relevant</u>, or <u>accurate evidence</u>. Evidence is <u>connected</u> across this TPE Domain

(2) Emerging—The candidate provides <u>partial evidence</u> demonstrating the competency or competencies. Candidate's practices demonstrate a preponderance of <u>minimal, limited, cursory, inconsistent</u>, and/or <u>ambiguous</u> evidence. Evidence is <u>weakly connected</u> across this TPE Domain and may be <u>inconsistent</u>.

(1) Beginning—The candidate provides <u>little or no evidence</u> demonstrating the competency or competencies. Candidate's practices demonstrate a preponderance of <u>inappropriate, irrelevant, inaccurate, or missing evidence</u>. Evidence is <u>unconnected</u> across the TPE Domain.

Activity	Integrating/Innovative 4	Applying 3	Emerging 2	Beginning 1
Introduction	Defines learning expectations clearly. Grade appropriate content. Establishes transfer to prior learning. Creates bridges from students' past learning. Clear rationale stated.	Defines learning expectations. Grade appropriate content. Establishes transfer to prior learning.	Limited definition of learning expectations. Grade appropriate content.	Minimal definition of learning expectations.
Learner Outcomes	States learner outcomes clearly. Learners have a clear understanding of what is expected of them. Learners can determine what they should know and be able to do as a result of the learning and instruction. Outcomes are measureable. Clear rationale stated.	States learner outcomes. Learners have an understanding of what is expected of them. Outcomes measureable.	States measureable learner outcomes.	Learner outcomes are not stated.
Pre-assessment Activity	Determines students' abilities and developmental needs. Prescribes instruction based on needs and IEPs. Considers a variety of student factors: e.g., linguistic background, academic language and abilities, content knowledge, cultural and health considerations, interests and aspirations, physical development, social development, emotional development. Clear rationale stated.	Determines students' abilities and developmental needs. Prescribes instruction based on needs and IEPs. Considers three student factors: e.g., linguistic background, academic abilities, social development.	Determines students' abilities and developmental needs. Prescribes instruction based on needs and IEPs. Considers one student factor: e.g., academic abilities.	Determines students' abilities and developmental needs. instruction does not meet student's abilities or developmental needs.
Differentiation, Adaptation & Accommodation Strategies	Modifies learning activities that provide accommodations and modifications for students with exception-alities and English language learners, at-risk students and gifted students. Rationale for the selection of the accommodations, modifications and differentiated strategies is identified.	Adapts learning activities to provide accommodations and modifications for two to three students with exceptionalities or other learning needs.	Adapts learning activities for one student that requires accommodations and modifications.	Modifications not evident.

Activity	Integrating/Innovative	Applying	Emerging	Beginning
	4	**3**	**2**	**1**
Resources	Prepares resources prior to instruction and readily available. Clearly relates resources to the learning outcome. Prepares resources to meet the varying skill levels and special needs of students. Distributes resources efficiently to provide maximum instructional time. Clear rationale stated.	Prepares resources prior to instruction and readily available. Resources are clearly related to the learning outcome. Prepares resources to meet some student's special learning needs. Distributes resources efficiently.	Prepares resources prior to instruction. Somewhat relates resources to the learning outcome. Meets one student's special learning needs with resources.	Resources are not prepared in advance of instruction. Resources not related to the learning outcome. No special needs material for accommodations evident.
Learning Activities: Explicit Teacher Instruction	Includes explicit teacher instruction: Explains, models, demonstrates, checks for understanding, Connects to students' interests, Highly creative, engaging learning activities, Clear rationale for selecting learning activities.	Includes explicit teacher instruction: Explains, models, demonstrates, checking for understanding, Creative engaging learning activities, Rationale for selecting learning activities.	Includes explicit teacher instruction: Explains, models and demonstrates, Learning activity, Limited rationale for selecting learning activity.	Includes explicit teacher instruction: Minimal explanation, modeling and/or demonstrating, No learning activity, No rationale provided.
Learning Activities: Guided Practice	Enthusiastic engagement in a creative, appropriate learning activity by students. e.g., writing prompt, oral debate, manipulating objects to solve a problem. Provides ongoing feedback to students and checks for understanding using questioning techniques and observation. Provides clear rationale for using the learning activity.	Engagement in an appropriate learning activity by students. Provides ongoing feedback to students. Provides an adequate rationale for using the learning activity.	Limited engagement in an appropriate learning activity by students. Provides limited feedback to students. Provides limited rationale for using the learning activity.	Minimal/no evidence of students understanding of the learning outcome and activity. Minimal/no evidence of teacher feedback to students. No rationale for using the learning activity.
Independent Practice	Assigns appropriate Independent Practice activity to further students understanding of learning outcome. Explains and models Independent Practice activity. Checks for understanding. Provides clear rationale for the Independent Practice activity.	Assigns appropriate Independent Practice activity. Explains the activity. Provides rationale for activity.	Assigns an Independent Practice activity. Provides limited rationale.	No Independent Practice activity assigned. Provides no rationale.

Activity	Integrating/Innovative	Applying	Emerging	Beginning
	4	**3**	**2**	**1**
Assessment and Evaluation	Uses a learning activity or assessment tool to determine student learning. Provides a variety of assessment adaptations and accommodations for students with exceptionalities. Evaluates student learning using assessment data. Prescribes further instruction based on data collection. Clear rationale stated.	Uses a learning activity or assessment tool to determine student learning. Provides assessment adaptation for one student. Evaluates student learning using assessment data.	Assesses student learning informally. Limited assessment adaptations or accommodations Limited data collection.	Minimal assessment of student learning. No assessment adaptations or accommodations. No data collection.
Closure	Students demonstrate a clear understanding of the learning outcome by sharing what they learned. Asks probing questions to stimulate the discussion, clarifies unanswered questions and determines students' understanding. Asks students to relate the importance of the learning outcome to their lives. Reflects on the students' understanding of the learning outcome based on their responses and determines future instructional focus. Clear rationale stated.	Students demonstrate an understanding of the learning outcome by sharing what they learned. Asks questions related to the learning outcome to determine students' understanding. Reflects on the students' understanding of the outcome based on their responses.	Students briefly shared what they learned. Asks a few questions related to the learning outcome.	Closure vague or not present in the lesson.
Scoring	Integrating/Innovative **Rubric Score 4**	Applying **Rubric Score 3**	Emerging **Rubric Score 2**	Beginning **Rubric Score 1**

Activity	Integrating/Innovative	Applying	Emerging	Beginning
	4	3	2	1
Oral Reflection/Assessment of Learning (Evaluated during post-observation conference)	Detailed lesson reflection: Clear description of what went well. Clear description of what could have been done differently based on students' response to the lesson? e.g. lesson strategies, classroom management procedures, etc. Clear description of what the assessment results indicated regarding student learning. Clear description of the next steps to be taken to ensure all students master the learning outcome.	Includes lesson reflection: Description of what went well. Description of what could have been done differently. Description of the assessment results. Description of what might occur in the future regarding the learning outcome.	Includes lesson reflection: Limited description of what went well. Limited description of what could have been done differently. Limited future instructional plans.	Reflection absent: Minimal/no description of what went well. Minimal/ no description of what could have been done differently. Minimal/no future instructional plans.

● **FIGURE A.1**

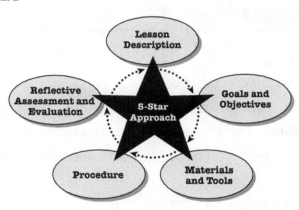

APPENDIX B

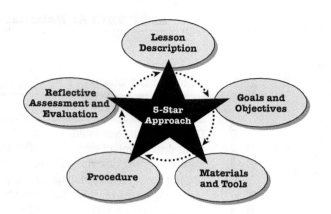

Practice: Analyzing Lesson Plans

Below you will find two sample lesson plans developed to demonstrate a variety of activities in the classroom. These plans are united by a common topic, goal and objectives, yet differ in purpose: the first is focused mainly on new material presentation, the second, however, targets knowledge construction and skill development. These two plans make up a unit. Analyze these lesson plans paying attention to how these plans are structured, what activities are used, and how students are guided to achieve the learning outcomes.

LESSON PLAN 1

1. DESCRIPTION

Date: September 6, 2012

Subject: Geography

Topic: The United States of America and its 50 states

Grade: 5th (26 students, diverse class with 7 ELL students)

2. GOALS AND OBJECTIVES

Goals: Enhance students' knowledge of the United States, to make students aware of the different states geographical boundaries, learn the names of 50 states and their capitals.

Objectives: Students will be able to:

1. Name the 50 states together with their abbreviations and their capitals

2. Find each of the states and their capitals on the map and describe their location

3. Recall basic facts of the states and share them in communication with peers

Standards: California History—Social Science Content Standard 3.1

Accommodations: Accommodations for students with special needs in this lesson may include the following adaptations to your methodological approach:

A. Adaptive equipment:

- Ramps into and out of classroom
- Hand or foot controls
- Adjustable tables
- Enlarged texts
- Audio texts

B. In your presentation remember to:

- Explain lesson's vocabulary
- Repeat concepts when necessary
- Sum up key points
- Enhance learning via audiovisual aids,
- Reflective assessments can be done orally and at end of lesson

Your curriculum objectives and outcomes might be adapted or supplemented to meet specific student needs. You should have an email and phone list to seek assistance available from:

- Special educators
- Special education aides
- Your district office
- Tutors
- Trained volunteers

Accommodations for ELL: Use the following support mechanisms when conducting specially designed academic instruction in English.

- Use a Model: Select samples of what an acceptable answer to a question or finished product might look like. Recall that 80 percent of teaching is modeling.

- Engage via Synthesis: Integrate a student's prior knowledge and build an analogy to construct a bridge of understanding to the student. Knowledge is associative, so seek connections with notions your students already possess.

- Employ Metacognition: Teach your students to "think about how they think." Knowing one's learning style can help any student in the process of mastering new skills and knowledge.

- Connect via Multisensory Approaches: Use as many of the five senses as possible to present students with clues via sound, text, image and tactile experiences and combine to interact with knowledge, learning tools and with other students.

Basic Vocabulary: Names of the 50 states and their capitals and the nation's capital District of Columbia (102 definitions in all).

3. MATERIALS AND TOOLS:

Texts: Social Studies textbook

Web links:

- States and capital—**http://www.50states.com/**
- Yahoo! Get Local—**http://dir.yahoo.com/Regional/U_S_States**
- All 50 American States Global—**http://www.globalcomputing.com/states.html**
- Color Landform Atlas of the United States—**http://fermi.jhuapl.edu/states/states.html**
- Stately Knowledge: Facts about the United States—**http://www.ipl.org/youth/stateknow/**
- US States Crossword Puzzle—**http://www.infoplease.com/states.html**

Visuals: a map of the USA, United States Mats, U.S.A. Map Puzzle, Novel Notes *US Map*, video *Travel Around the USA*

Technologies: DVD player or VCR and TV, CD player or tape recorder, computer with the Internet hookup, LCD projector.

Handouts: Lyrics of songs *The United States, States & Capitals, Rock'n Learn* from *National Geographic Journal*, World Wide Web.

4. PROCEDURE:

4.1 Introduction (3 min)

Last time we talked about our home town and state. Today we will talk about the geographic location of the United States. Where is our country located, on what continent? What are the two oceans that wash its shores? What countries are our neighbors to the north and to the south?

4.2. Teacher Presentation (20 min.)

Today we are going to travel around our nation. We will see how diverse it is. We will also learn that our nation consists of smaller parts called states. You may already know many of them.

Now let's play the Snowball game. One of you will give the name of one of the states. The second student will repeat this name and add another state. The third will repeat the first two names and add up one more name. So it will go around the class until you add no new names. Don't repeat the same name. Understand? Let's play!

Probing students' knowledge: You did a great job. How many states have we named? Do you know how many are there in all? So, how many more do we have to learn?

The teacher starts presentation of the new topic by asking the class questions:

- What state do we live in?
- What is the capital of our state?
- What are the neighboring states?
- Where are they located? Show on the map.
- What states have you been to?
- Do you know how many states there are?
- What is the capital of the United States?
- What in special federal district is the capital of the United States located?

Let's take a look at the map of the United States. As you can see, it is divided into many states.

Q: Do you remember how many states there are?

Ans. Correct, 50.

Q: What is a state?

Ans. Yes, a state in a part of the union which has boundaries and makes laws that do not conflict the federal law.

There are 48 states in situated together in continental part of North America, and two states are separated from the rest, Alaska also in North America, and Hawaii in the Pacific Ocean.

Q: What can you say looking at the shape of the states?

Ans. Yes, they have unusual shapes.

Q: Why, do you think this is so?

Ans. Right, rivers, lakes and mountains separate many of the states, and natural boundaries do not run in straight lines.

Q: Which is the largest state in territory?

Ans. Right Alaska

In population?

Ans. Right, California

Which is the smallest state in territory?

Ans. Rhode Island

In population?

Ans. Yes, Wyoming

Q: Do you know how many original states there were?

Ans. Right, 13.

Q: Do you know each state has an abbreviated name for convenience of use? What is the short for California, for example?

Ans. Yes, CA

The presentation is conducted in the form of the narration starting from mentioning our nation's capital, Washington, D.C., and ending in the students' home state. The teacher relates the information accompanying the story pointing to the states on the map. During the presentation, the teacher asks questions to maintain students' attention and check their knowledge and understanding.

4.3. Checking students' acquisition

The teacher checks understanding by asking questions:

* So, how many states are there in the USA?
* Which is the largest state in territory?
* Which is the largest state in population?
* Which is the smallest state in territory?
* Which is the smallest state in population?

4.4. Video demonstration (12 min.)

Now you are going to watch a short video *Around the United States* to once again go over what we have just learned. You will recognize the states and their names. Make a mental note of at least one specific characteristic of each of the states. After the video we will share our notes and impressions in the discussion.

Now, after we made a tour of our country, let's see what impressed you most. I'd like everybody to say a few words about the most interesting part of the video.

4.5. Singing the Song (7 min).

There have been quite a few songs composed about this country. Let's hear one of them and then you will receive the lyrics and we will sing it together. Later you will learn this song by heart.

Teaching tips: A fun way to learn the states and capitals of the United States is by singing songs. One resource which includes lyrics and recorded music is called *States & Capitals: Rock'n Learn.* The first song list the states in alphabetic order followed by their capitals. Students listen, rap along, and follow the lyrics in the book. The second song presents the states and their capitals in a mixed-up order. A longer delay allows more time for a student to sing along with the voice on tape. The third song gives practice naming the states aloud in each geographic region.

Teaching tip: Presentation is conducted in several cycles: a game of Snowball, questions to the class, teacher's narrative, then a video with a subsequent discussion, and finally singing a song.

Homework: **(2 min)**

- Make up a list of the most important state landmarks you know.
- Find out 10 important facts about one of the states (The states are distributed among students). Use the books in the school library and the Internet.
- Interview your parents about one of the states they have visited and write their story to read in class.
- Learn to sing the song about the US states and capitals.

Teaching tip: Homework can be given on individual pieces of paper.

Closure: **(1 min)**

Today we learned that out country consists of 50 states. Now we know some their names and their capitals. We also know where they are located and can find them on the map. Next time we will learn more about our great country.

5. REFLECTIVE ASSESSMENT AND EVALUATION:

1. Consider students' answers and comment
2. Keep a record of student participation
3. Note who is going to the chalk board (front of the class) and showing the states on the map.

Conferences: Meet with students on an on-going basis to discuss their strengths and weaknesses. Ask students how they plan to continue to improve.

LESSON PLAN 2 (Continuation of Lesson 1)

1. DESCRIPTION

Date: September 10, 2012

Subject: Geography

Topic: The United States of America and its 50 states

Grade: 5th (26 students, diverse class with 7 ELL students)

2. GOALS AND OBJECTIVES

Goals: Enhance students' knowledge of the United States so they increase their awareness of the different states geographical aspects.

Objectives: Students will be able to:

a. Improve reading and writing skills based on the lesson material and assignments

b. Develop computer and Internet skills, such as information search, selection, evaluation and storing

c. Demonstrate communication and collaboration skills in discussions and presentations to the class

Standards: California History—Social Science Content Standard 3.1

Accommodations (see Lesson 1)

3. MATERIALS AND TOOLS

Same as in Lesson 1.

4. PROCEDURE:

Introduction: (5 min)

Last time we have learned about 50 states. You are in the process of learning all their names and their capitals and in time will be able to locate them on the map. Teacher will review previous lesson.

Class Activities: (25 min)

1. Individual

• Make up a list of the states you have visited. Then read to the class.

• Write the names of the states where you have relatives, such as a grandmother or grandfather, an uncle or aunt or cousins. Share this information with your neighbor.

2. Small group

- A puzzle game. Put together the map of the country using a US map puzzle in groups of three.

- We will have 6 groups in class each group represents a different states. Each group will represent the Department of Tourism in their specific state government. As the different states have many places of natural beauty, landmarks, and historical sites, each group wishes to attract more tourists from all over the country as well as overseas to enjoy and educate themselves about the scenic wonders in the United States. The task will be to develop plans of how to attract more tourists to the states. One part of the project will be to prepare an advertisement that would describe the state in the most attractive way. So, develop a plan and write this ad. Then, present it to the class.

3. Whole class

- Let's play tennis. We will have two teams that will line up in two rows opposing each other. We will kick the ball in and decide who will start the game. Each of the teams will name one of the states in turn. The winning team will be the one that gives the last name. The conditions are not to give more than one name and not to repeat the same name. Clear? Let's start.

- Class project: Let's write a class book *The States of the Union* with pictures. We will distribute states among you, and each of you will write a description about one state. This report will have to tell us about its location, capital, landmarks, industry, state nickname, state bird and state animal, what grows and what is found underground. Find three pictures about your state and attach them to your report. Use the books in school library, *National Geographic* and Internet resources. After we collect all your reports, we will compile them into the book which all can share.

Homework: (2 min)

1. Write a report for the last project.
2. Send an electronic postcard to one of your class mates using the *1001 Postcards web site*.

Closure (1 min)

Today we learned more about the various states of union. Someday you may wish to take a vacation in a state you have described for out class. In addition, we began a class project *The States of the Union* in which all of us will share information about our nation.

5. REFLECTIVE ASSESSMENT AND EVALUATION:

1. Consider students answers and presentations
2. Test knowledge states and their capitals

Conferences: Meet with students on an on-going basis to converse about their comprehension (e.g. Before we finish our lesson, I will ask one of you to come out and tell what we have learn today about the US states, showing them on the map.)

Testing: (17 min)

Part 1 Matching (25 points)

Present students with two columns of 10 different states (in the right hand column) and their capitals (in the left hand column). Match the state with the capital by drawing a line from one to the other.

Part 2 Short Answer (75 points)

Based on your new knowledge explain, in at least 100 words, which state would you like to visit and why?

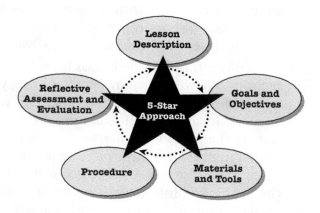

....

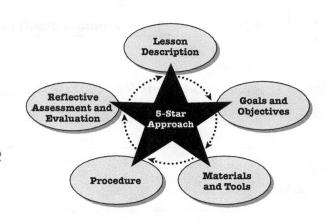

Lesson Plan Template

5-Star Lesson Plan Worksheet
....

1. DESCRIPTION

Date: _____

Subject: _____

Topic: _____

Grade: _____

2. GOALS AND OBJECTIVES

Goals: _____

_____

_____

Objectives: _____

_____

_____

Standards: _____

_____

_____

Accommodations for ELL/SDAIE: _____

_____

_____

Basic Vocabulary: _____

_____

_____

3. MATERIALS AND TOOLS

Texts: _____

_____

Visuals: _____

_____

Technologies: _____

_____

Handouts: _____

_____

4. PROCEDURE

Introduction (. . . min.): _____

_____

_____

Teacher Presentation (. . . min.): _____

_____

_____

*Class Activities (. . . min.):*_____

_____

_____

Homework (. . . min.): _____

_____

_____

Closure (. . . min.): _____

_____

_____

5. ASSESSMENT AND/OR EVALUATION

Conferences: _____

_____

_____

*Test:*_____

_____

_____

SUGGESTED READINGS

Lesson planning

Brunn, P. (2010). *The Lesson Planning Handbook: Essential Strategies That Inspire Student Thinking and Learning.* New York: Scholastic Teaching Resources.

Serdyukov, P., and Ryan, M. (2008). *Writing Effective Lesson Plans: The 5-star approach.* Boston: Allyn&Bacon.

Skowron, J. (2006). *Powerful Lesson Planning: Every Teacher's Guide to Effective Instruction.* Thousand Oaks, CA: Corwin Press.

General Issues

Aronson, J. (Ed.). (2002). *Improving academic achievement: Impact of psychological factors on education.* Boston: Academic Press.

Bloom, B., Engelhart, M., Furst, E., Hill, W. & Krathwohl, D. (1956). *Taxonomy of educational objectives: cognitive domain.* New York: Longman

Bloom's Taxonomy: http://www.coun.uvic.ca/learn/program/hndouts/bloom.html

Boyle-Baise, M. (2002). *Multicultural service learning: Educating teachers in diverse communities.* New York: Teachers College Press.

Christenson, S. L., & Sheridan, S. M. (2001). *Schools and families: Creating essential connections for learning.* New York: Guilford Press.

Cotton, K. (2000). *The schooling practices that matter most.* Alexandria, VA: Association for Supervision and Curriculum Development.

Effective lesson planning for English language learners by Jill Kerper Mora, Ed.D. San Diego State University. http://coe.sdsu.edu/people/jmora/MoraModules/ELLInstruction.htm#LessonPlan

Eggen, P.D., Kauchak, D.P. (2006). *Learning and teaching research-based methods.* Boston: Allyn and Bacon.

Ellison, L. (2001). *The personal intelligences: Promoting social and emotional learning.* Thousand Oaks, CA: Corwin Press.

Gardner, H. (1993). *Frames of mind: The theory of multiple intelligences.* (10th ed.). New York: Basic Books.

Gildner, C. (2001). *Enjoy teaching: Helpful hints for the classroom.* Lanham, MD: Scarecrow Education.

Gronlund, N. E., (2000) *Writing instructional objectives for teaching and assessment.* (7th ed.) Upper Saddle River, NJ: Merrill/Prentice Hall.

Harlan, J. C., & Rowland, S. T. (2002). *Behavior management strategies for teachers: Achieving instructional effectiveness, student success, and student motivation—every teacher and any student can.* Springfield, IL: Charles C. Thomas.

Hebert, E. A. (2001). *The power of portfolios: What children can teach us about learning and assessment.* San Francisco: Jossey-Bass.

Henze, R. (2002). *Leading for diversity: How school leaders promote positive interethnic relations.* Thousand Oaks, CA: Corwin Press.

Hopkins, D. (2001). *School improvement for real.* New York: Routledge.

Joyce, B., & Weil, M. with Calhoun, E. (2004). *Models of teaching.* (7th ed.) Needham Heights, MA: Allyn and Bacon.

Kane, C. (1994). *Prisoners of time.* Report of the National Education Commission on Time and Learning. April 1994. http://ed.gov/pubs/PrisonersOfTime/Prisoners.html

Kleinert, H. L., & Kearns, J. (2001). *Alternate assessment: Measuring outcomes and supports for students with disabilities.* Baltimore, MD: P.H. Brookes Pub. Co.

Lasley, T. J., Matczynski, T. J., & Rowley, J. (2002). *Instructional models: Strategies for teaching in a diverse society.* Belmont, CA: Wadsworth/Thomson Learning

Levin, B. (2001). *Reforming education: From origins to outcomes.* New York: Routledge/Falmer.

Mager, R. (1962). *Preparing instructional objectives.* Palo Alto: Fearon Publishers, Inc.

Marjoribanks, K. (2002). *Family and school capital: Towards a context theory of students' school outcomes.* Boston: Kluwer Academic Publishers.

McMillan, J. H. (2001). *Classroom assessment: Principles and practice for effective instruction.* Boston: Allyn and Bacon.

Metzker, B. (2003) Time and learning. *ERIC Digest* ED474260 http://eric.ed.gov/ERICDocs/data/ericdocs2/content_storage_01/0000000b/80/2a/38/d8.pdf

Midgley, C. (Ed.). (2002). *Goals, goal structures, and patterns of adaptive learning.* Mahwah, NJ: Lawrence Erlbaum.

Naparstek, N. (2002). *Successful educators: A practical guide for understanding children's learning problems and mental health issues.* Westport, CT: Bergin & Garvey.

Orlich, D.C., Harder, R.J., Callahan, R.C., Gibson, H.W. (2001). *Teaching strategies: A guide to better instruction.* Boston: Houghton Mifflin Company.

Parsons, B. A. (2002). *Evaluative inquiry: Using evaluation to promote student success.* Thousand Oaks, CA: Corwin Press.

Queen, J. A. (2003). *The block scheduling handbook.* Thousand Oaks, CA: Corwin Press.

Ryan, M., (2007). *Ask the teacher: A practitioner's guide to teaching and learning in the diverse classroom.* Boston, MA: Allyn and Bacon

Scott, P. & Conrad, C. (1992). A critique of intensive courses and an agenda for research. *Higher education: Handbook of theory and research*, NY: Agathod Press.

Slavin, R. E., & Madden, N. A. (Eds.). (2001). *Success for all: Research and reform in elementary education.* Mahwah, NJ: L. Erlbaum Associates.

Serdyukov, P. (2002) *Lesson plan: A teacher's guide.* Boston: Pearson Education.

Serdyukov, P., and Hill, R. (2004). Masonry of E-learning: Managing Knowledge Construction and Skill Development in an Online Course. *Proceedings of E-Learn World Conference on E-Learning in Corporate, Government, Healthcare, & Higher Education*, Washington, D.C., November 2004.

Serdyukov, P. (2005) *Effective lesson planning.* In: Lessow-Hurley, J. (2005). *The foundations of dual language instruction* (4th ed.), with Serdyukov, P. (2004). *Effective lesson planning.* (3rd ed.) Boston: Addison Wesley Longman, Inc.

Serdyukov, P. and Serdyukova, N. (2006). Time efficiency of online learning. *Proceedings of The 22nd ICDE World Conference*, September 3-6, 2006 in Rio de Janeiro, Brazil.

Schwartz, P., & Webb, G. (Eds.). (2002). *Assessment: Case studies, experience and practice.* London: Kogan Page.

Siraj-Blatchford, I., & Clarke, P. (2000). *Supporting identity, diversity, and language in the early years.* Philadelphia, PA: Open University Press.

Stefanakis, E. H. (2002). *Multiple intelligences and portfolios: A window into the learner's mind.* Portsmouth, NH: Heinemann.

Vygotsky, L.S. (1978). *Mind in society: The development of higher psychological processes* (M. Cole, V. John-Steiner, S. Scribner, & E. Souberman, Eds. and Trans.). Cambridge, MA: Harvard University Press.

Walker, Wilson, L. (2002). *Better instruction through assessment: What your students are trying to tell you.* Larchmont, NY: Eye on Education.

Web links:

http://ericir.syr.edu/ A library of lesson plans created by teachers

Kizlik, B. Lesson Planning, Lesson Plan Formats and Lesson Plan Ideas. http://www.adprima.com/lesson.htm

The Gateway to Educational Materials http://www.thegateway.org

Developing Learning Outcomes. http://www.stedwards.edu/cte/learningout.htm

Instructional Planning Template http://wwwbel.lkwash.wednet.edu/NAESP/template.html

Ask ERIC Lesson Plans http://www.askeric.org/Virtual/Lessons/

Busy Teachers' WebSite K-12 http://www.ceismc.gatech.edu/busyt

CEC Lesson Plans http://www.col-ed.org/cur/

CNN/AOL @ School http://school.aol.com/teachers/lesson_plans.adp

EdHelper www.edhelper.com/

Education World Lesson Planning Center http://www.education-world.com/a_lesson/

Effective Lesson Planning for English Language Learners http://coe.sdsu.edu/people/jmora/5StepELL/Default.htm

ENCARTA lesson collection http://encarta.msn.com/schoolhouse/default.asp

English Companion http://www.englishcompanion.com/

ERIC/CLL Language Link http://www.cal.org/ericcll/

LessonPlanners.com http://www.lessonplanners.com/

Lesson Plans and Projects. AOL School http://school.aol.com/teachers/lesson_plans.adp

Lesson Plans and Teaching strategies http://www.csun.edu/~hcedu013/plans.html#Lesson%20Plans

Lesson Plans at Teachnet www.teachnet.com/lesson.html

Lesson plans by Gibson Associates http://www.netcore.ca/~gibsonjs/gaweb1.htm

LessonPlansPage.com http://www.lessonplanspage.com/

PBS Teacher Source http://www.pbs.org/
teachersource/search.htm

SDAIE Handbook: Techniques, Strategies, and Suggestions for Teachers of LEP and Former LEP Students http://www.csupomona.edu/~tassi/sdaie.htm

Some Basic Lesson Presentation Elements
http://www.humboldt.edu/~tha1/hunter-eei.html

Teachers' Net Lesson Bank http://teachers.net/
lessons/

Teachers.net http://teachers.net/lessons

TESL-EJ. Teaching English as a Second or Foreign Language. An International Journal. http://www
-writing.berkeley.edu/TESL-EJ/index.html

Zoom School http://www.enchantedlearning
.com/school/index.shtml

GLOSSARY

Accommodation A concept that helps ensure the learning process for every student. The authors use the most encompassing view of the notion of inclusion to cover all students. Accommodation includes content adaptation, special strategies, such as vocabulary work before new material presentation to help ELL students, slow but natural speech, clear enunciation, short, simple sentences, visual reinforcement and frequent comprehension checks.

Activity A student action targeting a certain knowledge and/or skill. This concept functions to implement a strategy. A strategy in action is an activity. For example, listening, speaking, reading, writing, dancing and singing can all be activities that forward a given conceptual strategy.

Affective domain A realm of learning involves our emotions and values. Inspiration, motivation and empowerment, all affective in nature, express our deepest feelings of self-worth and commitment. One's affective disposition is interwoven into one's cognitive ability. A teacher's natural disposition, supportive and caring attitude towards students, positive environment, music, visuals, the atmosphere of joy and achievement are some affective factors.

Algorithm A procedure (a finite set of predetermined instructions) for accomplishing a given task which will end in a predefined outcome. Algorithms often have steps that repeat (iterate) or require making decisions using the "If . . . then . . . ." logical formula. There are three basic forms of an algorithm: linear, branching or iterative. A lesson plan can be presented as an algorithm as it moves step-by-step from one activity to another.

Assessment An appraisal of the learner which is inherently reflective. It is derived from the Latin *assessio*, which literally means, "to sit beside." If one can imagine an examiner sitting alongside a student and providing feedback (based on observing, documenting and analyzing the learner's work), we can better understand how the student is to accomplish genuine *assessment*, which is truly self-*assessment*.

Basic vocabulary Information made meaningful to every student by defining ideas and activities via a fundamental terminology. Actually, it is a minimal set of words necessary for a student to understand a particular topic.

Classroom activities Behaviors through which students perform various assignments, individual or collaborative, among which are: problem-solving, case studies, discussions, exercises, role playing, experimenting and presenting. These activities may be of at least two levels of complexity: basic (teacher guided exercises) and advanced (independent from teacher).

Class section A course populated with a finite number of students and scheduled as an autonomous unit within a program.

Closure A phase that incorporates the review of the lesson and the summary of the lesson's key points. It also includes general appraisal (assessment and evaluation) of the students' work and a short preview of the lesson to come.

Constructivism A learning theory based on the notion of building up one's own knowledge via the interaction between prior knowledge and new knowledge. Most effective knowledge is constructed in collaboration with peers under the guidance of an expert (teacher).

Course An instructional unit that delivers a certain subject matter or specific content representing a particular area that can be considered as a whole. A given subdivision of a discipline, which begins with the preview of a new plan, contains activities necessary to achieve the predefined outcomes, and ends with a general reflective review.

Curriculum The concept of what is to be taught to prepare students for given purpose. It contains content areas that are interrelated and interdependent.

Discipline An educational subject matter division (e.g. history, science, foreign language).

Educational technology   Technical, programming and instructional tools used together with human resources in teaching and learning.

Email   A communication tool for individual and group message exchange. At the same time, it is a great instrument for reading and writing instruction, individual and group tutoring and consultations, question and answer exercises, problem-solving and role playing.

Evaluation   A one-time glimpse of a student's knowledge expressed in a score, ranking, or grade that exists at a given point in time.

Gestalt   An overview an idea based on a holistic organizing principle or pattern.

Goal   A concept that represents the strategic, ultimate aim or purpose as given in the lesson.

Handouts   Tangible material given to students that can extend on or enhance the curriculum.

Homework   An extension of the school day via home study, which is vital for providing further independent learning, real-life applications and experiences. It is also needed for assuring retention.

Homework checkup   A stage in the lesson during which the students present their assigned out-of-class work, either by making oral presentations, or by turning in written work. It is important that the students realize that "we don't do disposable work."

Instructional tool   Anything that facilitates teaching and learning. We know that a fork or chopsticks are tools for eating. A book, magic marker, computer, or software program are all examples of instructional tools.

Introduction   The initial part or phase of the lesson intended to prepare students for learning by warming up, general conversation, reviewing the previous lesson's key points, setting the objectives and presenting the plan of the current lesson.

Iteration   A repeated procedure intended to bring the student competence to a predetermined level of the learning outcomes.

Lesson plan   A systemic, research-based sequence of instructional events to be implemented in a lesson. A lesson plan is the foundation of successful student learning, accurate assessment, and effective classroom management. It is essential in almost any aspect of daily classroom life. Most importantly, a well-constructed lesson plan sets a pathway to learning for your students.

Lesson planning   A regular teacher activity intended to prepare quality instruction. It helps to structure instruction, learning, classroom practice, and your time. It eventually makes your teaching performance more efficient, less stressful and, rewarding to you.

Lesson plan description   A formal part of the lesson plan containing all the essential information about lesson plan: the date of the lesson, the topic, subject area, grade, goals and objectives, standards, and rationale.

Lessons in a course   Constituent parts of the course, each being derived from another and dependent on the others. In the instructional process they extend sequentially through a certain period of time (a year, a semester, a quarter, a month, a week or a day) and together form a complete single whole, both as a system and as a continuum.

Manipulatives   Items to aid the learning process. For example, objects commonly used build structures as with blocks, to test recollection as with flash cards, or to count up tangible sums as with beans.

Materials   Anything carrying information or used for constructing knowledge and developing skills, (e.g. texts, video clips or any other information format, visuals). Visuals may include drawings, pictures, posters, handouts. In addition materials include realia, resources for drawing, coloring, constructing, such as paper, clay, fabric, or cardboard.

Method   A concept that represents theoretical instructional approach. For example, one can practice the communicative approach, accelerated learning, or cooperative learning. All are considered methodological in nature.

Modeling   The application of a prototype for instructional purposes it encourages following selected paradigms to facilitate learning. The teacher is the preeminent behavioral model for his and her students. Also called simulation, it is another aspect of organizing and structuring. When you prepare a lesson plan, you actually create a model, an organizational structure of an instructional process.

Motivation   A driving force in student learning; closely connected to the affective domain. Two types of motivation are known: extrinsic and intrinsic, the latter being the more efficient and more powerful of the two.

Objective   A concept that represents one of the explicit, intermediate aims that helps achieve the specific pre-designed outcomes of the lesson. The objectives for the lesson plan are determined by the broader goals of the lesson. Objectives are constituent parts of the goal. Actually, objectives are the lesson's projected outcomes.

Outcomes   The implemented objectives achieved through effective instruction and students' learning.

Plan A systematic means to reach an end.

Presentation   A phase of the lesson in which the new material is introduced by the teacher in direct instruction or from another source. Often the teacher uses various visuals germane to the area of study.

Prior knowledge   The understanding that students bring to classroom. New knowledge begins to be understood when the learner uses his or her prior knowledge to make out familiar patterns of thought within the new knowledge in order to interpret new or enhanced meanings. Within the constructivist framework, prior knowledge is a significant factor in the learning process.

Procedure   A critical part of any lesson in which the teacher and students interact, communicate, share information, solve problems and do assignments to achieve the lesson goals and objectives. Procedures assist in the construction of knowledge and its retention, and in skill application and development

Professional competence   The ability to professionally perform on the job.

Realia   Various real-life objects that help make learning realistic. They may include price lists from the stores to be used in math class, menus from restaurants in ESL lessons on ordering food, a collection of rocks in a geology class, chemical compounds for chemistry experiments.

Socratic seminars   A method to move from the unexamined to the examined by participating in a dialogue about a specific idea or text. Thoughtful conversation is dependent on higher order critical thinking in the search for meaning rather than the regurgitation of information.

Spiral curriculum   A concept of revisiting learned concepts at increased levels of sophistication.

Standard   Identified subject area content which may be aligned with test content. Academic standards define both breadth and depth. State standards typically delineate anticipated outcomes. In simple terms they state what students are required to know and what students should be able to perform.

Strategic planning   Designing a course in a particular subject area.

Strategy   Particular implementation of a method that operates through specially organized instructional activities.

Structured classroom activity   A major element of your plan and a basic unit of organized learning.

Tactical planning   Daily instruction design focusing on immediate tasks including lesson planning.

Technology   A sophisticated tool, usually an electronic, mechanical or optical device.

Technology applications Special instructional uses of technology in teaching and learning.

Time This is a most significant concept for teacher and a learner; implies changes in curricular and methodological considerations. Time affects your lesson planning

Tools The teacher's and student's instruments that can be non-technological, such as chalkboard, ruler, textbooks, dictionaries, reference books, and technological which means they are based on electronics, mechanics, and optics, such as computers, calculators, DVD players, overhead projectors, computer programs, and Internet.

INDEX